color

&type

Working

with

Computer

Type

3

The author and publisher dedicate this book to
their very good friend and mentor, Jean Koefoed,
without whom this series would not have been
created. The recent loss of such a fine publisher
and professional in the Graphic Arts field will
surely be felt throughout our industry. We mourn
him but rejoice in the privilege of having known
and worked with him.

RC/BM 9 Oct 96

A RotoVision Book
Published and Distributed by RotoVision SA
7 rue du Bugnon
1299 Crans
Switzerland

RotoVision SA Sales Office
Sheridan House
112/116A Western Road
Hove,West Sussex BN3 1DD
England
Tel   44 1273 72 72 68
Fax   44 1273 72 72 69

Distributed to the trade in the United States by

Watson Guptill Publications
1515 Broadway
New York, New York 10036

ISBN 2-88046-278-9

Book design by Rob Carter

Production and separations in Singapore by

ProVision Pte. Ltd.
Tel   65 334 7720
Fax   65 334 7721

Working with

Computer Type

3

Rob Carter

ROTOVISION

color&type

Contents

Working with color and type poses numerous challenges. Paying attention to all of the minute but critical details in type such as typeface selection and spacing requires sensitivity, patience, and practice. When color and type join forces, the challenges are significantly magnified. Color should not only be chosen to create a desired effect or mood; it should also be chosen with typographic legibility in mind. We are accustomed to seeing black type on white paper, and traditionally this combination is most readable. From the moment color is added to either type or its background, legibility is compromised. As a result, the designer's task is to juggle the properties of both color and type, thus optimizing their communicative potential. Arm in arm, color and type are capable of breathing life into otherwise dull communication.

Prior to the onslaught of desktop computers, designers selected color from swatchbooks and color charts that offered a relatively limited palette of colors. Now the designer is able to select millions of colors from electronic palettes that can be accessed instantaneously. The sheer number of color choices is overwhelming. With innumerable fonts and a tremendous number of colors available on the desktop, how does one begin the complicated process of meaningfully combining type

and color on the desktop? What factors specific to combining type and color should you consider, and how do you know when the type and color combinations you have chosen are the right ones? *Working with Computer Type: Type and Color* tackles these questions and others, offering a practical guide for art directors, graphic designers, and desktop publishers at all levels.

The book is a guide for working with color and type, as well as a practical tool for selecting color combinations for type. A panorama of type and color specimens based on basic color schemes derived from the color wheel provides an invaluable guide for selecting your own type and color combinations. 30 case studies reveal how some of the world's leading graphic designers integrate type and color, use color as a communicative element, and create color schemes for expressive and communicative purposes. While the book focuses on printed communication, the timeless concepts presented apply also to electronic and interactive applications.

Some things never change, and in the typographic realm, principles upon which sound practice relies have remained essentially the same for centuries.

Some things never change, and in the typographic realm, principles upon which sound practice relies have remained essentially the same for centuries. These principles have over time developed in response to the way in which we read – the way in which we visually perceive the letters and words on a page. Working effectively with computer type (or working with type using any tool, for that matter) requires a solid knowledge of these typographic fundamentals. The following pages provide the reader with the basic vocabulary needed for informed practice, and a fuller understanding and appreciation of the case studies presented within this book.

The anatomy of type

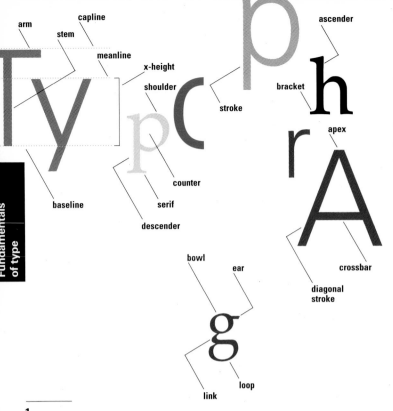

Diagram labels (fig. 1): arm, capline, stem, meanline, x-height, shoulder, stroke, ascender, bracket, apex, crossbar, diagonal stroke, counter, serif, baseline, descender, bowl, ear, loop, link, eye

1

The colorful terms used to describe type are not unlike the terms used to describe the parts of our own bodies. Letters have arms, legs, eyes, spines, and a few other parts, such as tails and stems, that we fortunately do not possess. These are the parts that have historically been used to construct letterforms. Learning this vocabulary can help the designer gain appreciation for the complexity of our alphabet, which at first glance appears very simple (fig. **1**). The structure of letters within the alphabet remains constant regardless of typeface. An upper-case *B,* for example, consists of one vertical and two curved strokes. These parts, however, may be expressed very differently from typeface to typeface (fig. **2**).

BB *B* B **B** B

2

Type classification

An inexhaustible variety of type styles is available for use today, and many attempts to classify these into logical groupings have fallen short due to the overlapping visual traits of typefaces. A flawless classification system does not exist; however, a general system based on the historical development of typefaces is used widely. This delineation breaks down typefaces into the following groups: Old Style, Transitional, Modern, Slab Serif (also called Egyptian), Sans Serif, and Display (fig. **3**).

The typographic font

In desktop publishing, the terms typeface and font are often used synonymously; however, a typeface is the design of characters unified by consistent visual properties, while a font is the complete set of characters in any one design, size, or style of type. These characters include but are not limited to upper- and lower-case

Old Style characteristics:
**Medium stroke contrast
Slanted stress
Oblique, bracketed serifs
Medium overall weight**

Transitional characteristics:
**Medium to high stroke contrast
Nearly vertical stress
Sharp, bracketed serifs
Slightly slanted serifs**

Modern characteristics:
**High stroke contrast
Vertical stress
Thin serifs
Serifs sometimes unbracketed**

Egyptian characteristics:
**Little stroke contrast
Little or no stress
Thick, square serifs
Large x-height**

Sans serif characteristics:
**Some stroke contrast
Nearly vertical stress
Squarish, curved strokes
Lower-case *g* has open tail**

Display typefaces do not possess a fixed number of characteristics.

Old Style

Transitional

Modern

Slab serif

Sans serif

Display

3

letters, numerals, small capitals, fractions, ligatures (two or more characters linked together into a single unit), punctuation, mathematical signs, accents, monetary symbols, and miscellaneous dingbats (assorted ornaments or fleurons designed for use in a font). Supplementing some desktop fonts are expert sets, which include characters such as small caps, a good selection of ligatures, fractions, and nonaligning figures. Minion Regular provides an excellent example of a font and its attendant expert set (fig. **4**).

The type family

A type family is a group of typefaces bound together by similar visual characteristics. Members of a family (typefaces) resemble one another, but also have their own unique visual traits. Typefaces within families consist of different weights and widths. Some type families consist of many members; others are composed of just a few. Extended families such as Stone include both serif and sans serif variations (fig. **5**).

Typographic measurement

The two primary units of measure in typography are the pica and the point. There are approximately six picas or 72 points to an inch; there are twelve points to a pica (fig. **6**). Points are used to specify the size of type, which includes the cap height of letters, plus a small interval of space above and below the letters. Typefaces of the same size may in fact appear different in size, depending on the size of the x-height. At the same size, letters with large x-heights appear larger than letters with smaller x-heights. Points are also used to measure the distance between lines; picas are used to measure the lengths of lines. The unit, a relative measure determined by dividing the em (which is the square of the type size), is used to reduce or increase the amount of space between

abcdefghijklmnopqrstuvwxyz
ABCDEFGHIJKLMNOPQRSTUVWXYZ&
ABCDEFGHIJKLMNOPQRSTUVWXYZ&
(.;:,!?“”'’‘’~″‴‵‶′″˝˜ˆˇ ~'''《》〈〉- – —)
1234567890 1234567890 ($^{1234567890}/_{1234567890}$)
¼⅓½⅔¾⅝⅞%‰ [+√π=≠±≤≥÷∞°]
fffiflffifflŒßæœ $£§¢
ÂÅÁÇÎÏØÓÒÔÚ áéíóúåäëïöüàèìòùâêîû
¶‡†•⋆∧ ©™@

4

Stone Serif

Regular
Regular Italic
Semibold
Semibold Italic
Bold
Bold Italic

Stone Sans

Regular
Regular Italic
Semibold
Semibold Italic
Bold
Bold Italic

5

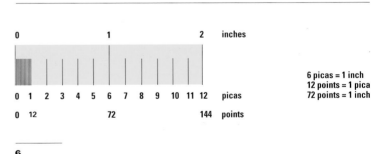

6 picas = 1 inch
12 points = 1 pica
72 points = 1 inch

6

letters, a process called tracking. Adjusting the awkward space between two letters to create consistency within words is called kerning.

The typographic grid

A typographic grid is used to aid the designer in organizing typographic and pictorial elements on a page and establishing unity among all of the parts of a design. Grids vary in complexity and configuration depending upon the nature of the information needing accommodation, and the physical properties of the typographic elements. Standard typographic grids possess flow lines, grid modules, text columns, column intervals, and margins (fig. **7**).

If the goal when working with type is to make it more readable, then heeding established legibility guidelines is of utmost importance. Departure from these "rules" should be attempted only after a designer is totally familiarized with them, and when content lends itself to expressive interpretation. Legibility represents those visual attributes in typography that make type readable.

Choosing typefaces

The first step in making type legible is to choose text typefaces that are open and well proportioned, typefaces that exhibit the regularity of classical serif faces, such as Baskerville, Bembo, Bodoni, Garamond; and the sans serif faces Franklin Gothic, Frutiger, and Gill Sans (fig. **8**). Typefaces with visual quirks, stylistic affectations, and irregularities among characters are less legible. Typefaces such as these may be fine, however, when used as display type.

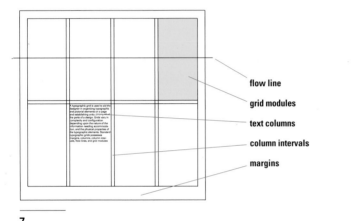

flow line

grid modules

text columns

column intervals

margins

7

Serif	Sans serif
Bembo	Franklin Gothic
Baskerville	Frutiger
Bodoni	Futura
Century Expanded	Gill Sans
Garamond	Helvetica

8

Type size, line length, and line spacing

Text that flows naturally when read is achieved when a harmonious relationship exists between type size, line length, and the spaces between lines of type (line spacing or leading). Even well-designed typefaces suffer from legibility impairment when just one of these aspects is out of balance. An adjustment to one of these factors usually requires an adjustment to one or more of the others.

Continuous text type that is too large or too small easily tires the reader. Optimum sizes for text type are between 8 and 11 points. Also, typefaces with a relatively large x-height improve readability.

Overly long or short lines of type also tire the reader and destroy a pleasant reading rhythm. Long lines are burdensome and tedious, whereas short lines cause choppy eye movements. Paying attention to the number of characters per line is a key in determining appropriate line lengths. It is generally agreed that lines of type consisting of a maximum of sixty or seventy characters promote readability (fig. **9**).

Line spacing ensures that the reader is not distracted by lines of type that visually run together. Without adequate space between lines, the eye struggles to distinguish one line from the next. Where lines are too widely spaced, the reader has trouble locating the next line. For optimum sizes of text type (8-11 points), one to four points of line spacing can help the reader easily discern each line, thus improving readability (fig. **10**).

8/9
Line spacing ensures that the reader is not distracted by lines of type that visually run together. With inadequate space between lines, the eye struggles to distinguish one line from the next. Where lines are too widely spaced, the reader has trouble locating the next line. For optimum sizes of text type (8-11 points), one to four points of line

8/11
Line spacing ensures that the reader is not distracted by lines of type that visually run together. With inadequate space between lines, the eye struggles to distinguish one line from the next. Where lines are too widely spaced, the reader has trouble locating the next line. For

8/10
Line spacing ensures that the reader is not distracted by lines of type that visually run together. With inadequate space between lines, the eye struggles to distinguish one line from the next. Where lines are too widely spaced, the reader has trouble locating the next line. For optimum sizes of text type (8-11

8/12
Line spacing ensures that the reader is not distracted by lines of type that visually run together. With inadequate space between lines, the eye struggles to distinguish one line from the next. Where lines are too widely spaced, the reader has trouble locating the next line. For

10

Overly long or short lines of type also tire the reader and destroy a pleasant reading rhythm. Long lines are burdensome and tedious, whereas short lines cause choppy eye movements. Paying attention to the number of characters per line is a key in determining appropriate line lengths. It is generally agreed that lines of type consisting of a maximum of sixty or seventy characters promote readability.

Overly long or short lines of type also tire the reader and destroy a pleasant reading rhythm. Long lines are burdensome and tedious, whereas short lines cause choppy eye movements. Paying attention to the number of characters per line is a key in determining appropriate line lengths. It is

Letter spacing

A number of factors determines correct letter spacing, including the typeface used, and the size and weight of the type. Consistent letter spacing provides an even typographic "color," a term referring to the texture and overall lightness or darkness of text. Consistent and even color is an attribute that enhances readability. Tighter letter spacing darkens the text, as in this sentence. L o o s e r l e t t e r s p a c i n g l i g h t e n s t h e t e x t. Pushed to either extreme, text becomes less readable. The chosen effect can enliven a page and enhance communication.

Word spacing

Word spacing should be proportionally adjusted to letter spacing so that letters flow gracefully and rhythmically into words, and words into lines. Too much word spacing destroys the even texture desired in text and causes words to become disjointed, as in this sentence. Toolittlewordspacing causeswordstobumpintooneanother. Either condition is hard on the reader.

Weight

The overall heaviness or lightness of the strokes composing type can affect readability. For typefaces that are too heavy, counters fill in and disappear. Typefaces that are too light are not easily distinguished from their background. Typefaces of contrasting weight are effectively used to create emphasis within text.

Width

Narrow typefaces are effectively used where there is an abundance of text, and space must be preserved. But readability is diminished when letters are too narrow (condensed) or too wide (expanded). Condensed letters fit nicely into narrow columns.

Italics

Italic and oblique type should be used with prudence, for large amounts of slanted characters set into text impede reading. Italics are best suited to create emphasis within text rather than to function as text.

Capitals versus lower case

TEXT SET IN ALL CAPITAL LETTERS NOT ONLY CONSUMES MORE SPACE THAN TEXT SET IN LOWER CASE, IT SEVERELY RETARDS THE READING PROCESS. LOWER-CASE LETTERS IMBUE TEXT WITH VISUAL CUES CREATED BY AN ABUNDANCE OF LETTER SHAPES, ASCENDERS, DESCENDERS, AND IRREGULAR WORD SHAPES. TEXT SET IN ALL CAPITALS IS VOID OF THESE CUES, FOR IT LACKS THIS VISUAL VARIETY.

Serif versus sans serif

Because of the horizontal flow created by serifs, it was thought at one time that serif typefaces were more readable than sans serif typefaces. Legibility research, however, reveals little difference between them. Sensitive letter spacing is a more important consideration.

Justified versus unjustified

Text can be aligned in five different ways: flush left, ragged right; flush right, ragged left; justified; centered; asymmetrically.

Flush left, ragged right text produces very even letter and word spacing, and because lines of type terminate at different points, the reader is able to easily locate each new line. This is per-haps the most legible means of aligning text.

Flush right, ragged left alignments work against
the reader by making it difficult to find each
new line. This method is suitable for small
amounts of text, but is not recommended for
large amounts.

Justified text (text aligned both left and right) can be very readable if the designer ensures that the spacing between letters and words is consistent, and that awkward gaps called "rivers" do not interrupt the flow of the text. Desktop publishing software enables the designer to fine tune the spacing.

Centered alignments give the text a very formal
appearance and are fine when used minimally.
But setting large amounts of text in this way
should be avoided.

Asymmetrical alignments
are used when the designer
wishes to

break
the text down into logical   "thought units,"

or to give the page
a more expressive appearance.
Obviously,
setting large amounts of text
in this manner

will tire the reader.

Color is visual magic, a language of illusion. Color is also reflected light, and as lighting conditions change, so does color. This explains why as night falls colors fade, and why the colors of a landscape vary significantly when viewed at different times of the day.

Color is visual magic, a language of illusion. Color is also reflected light, and as lighting conditions change, so does color. This explains why as night falls colors fade, and why the colors of a landscape vary significantly when viewed at different times of the day. When we see a color, what we actually see is an object that absorbs certain wavelengths of light and reflects others back to our eyes. For example, a red object absorbs all of the light rays except the red rays which are filtered back to the eyes. Black objects absorb all of the light rays, reflecting none back to our eyes; white objects absorb no rays, reflecting all of them back to our eyes. This phenomenon was first revealed in 1666 by Isaac Newton who found that by passing a beam of white light through a prism, he could break it up into the familiar spectrum of rainbow colors: violet, indigo, blue, green, yellow, orange, and red. We are most familiar with this spectrum, and the human eye easily perceives it. In reality, the spectral colors consist of a vast array of hues, each corresponding to a specific wavelength of light.

This chapter reviews basic color theory, and defines important color terms. For the beginner, it lays a solid foundation for building a deeper knowledge of color. For the professional designer and desktop publisher, it provides a welcome review. Learning to see color and obtaining an understanding of its inherent properties are the first steps to working effectively with color and type.

The color wheel

The color wheel is a helpful tool that shows the basic organization and interrelationships of colors. It is also used as a tool for color selection. This color wheel provides basic color terminology that anyone working with type and color should be completely familiar with. Many color wheel models exist, and some are quite complex. This wheel consists of 12 basic colors (fig. **1**). It is conceivable for a wheel to consist of an infinite number of variations, too subtle for the human eye to discern. Contained within the circle of color is a square of black, which is obtained by mixing together all of the surrounding colors. Though this color wheel consists of only 12 colors, it is the root of all other colors, a pure statement of chromatic harmony, and a fountain of imagination and emotion.

1

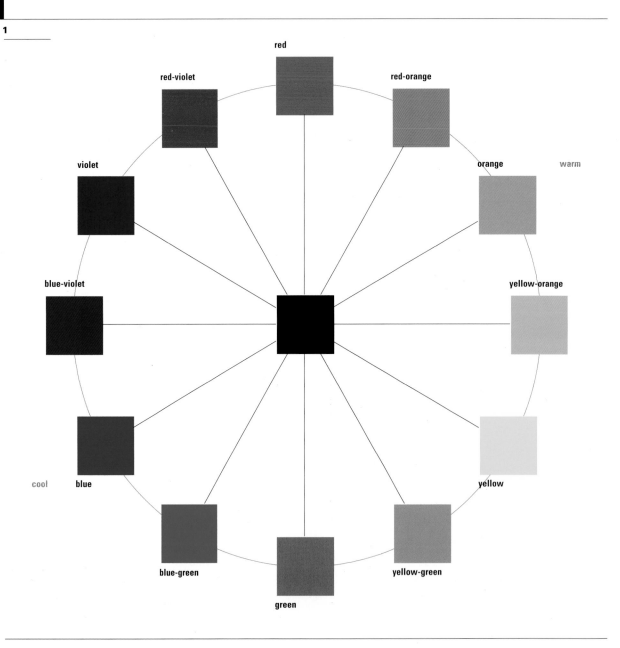

red

red-violet

red-orange

violet

orange

warm

blue-violet

yellow-orange

cool　blue

yellow

blue-green

yellow-green

green

Properties of color

hue
hue
hue

Three different sets of primary hues are accepted for use in different disciplines. The first set consists of red, yellow and blue and is used by artists and designers. Pigments of these colors can be mixed to obtain all other colors (top). The second set of primaries are red, green and blue. Called the additive primaries, these are the primaries of light and are used in science. These are also the colors found on the computer screen. When these colors are added together in different amounts they form all other colors; when added together equally they produce white light (middle). The third set consists of magenta, yellow, and cyan. These are the subtractive primaries and are used by printers. In printing, color separations are made by using filters to subtract light from the additive primaries, resulting in the subtractive process printing colors (bottom).

3

Hue

Hue is simply another name for color. The pure hues are identified by familiar names such as red, violet, green, purple, yellow. In the world of commercial products and pigments, hues have been given thousands of names. Desert Rose, Winter, Woodland Green, Apache Red, and African Violet may evoke romantic and exotic thoughts, but these names, aside from their marketing value, have little to do with the composition of the colors they represent. In reality, few legitimate names exist for hues. The basic twelve-color wheel pictured on the opposite page features the primary hues red, yellow, and blue; the secondary hues orange, green, and violet; and the six tertiary hues red-orange, orange-yellow, yellow-green, blue-green, blue-violet, and red-violet (fig. **2**). The secondary hues are obtained by mixing equal amounts of two primaries; the tertiary hues are acquired by mixing equal amounts of a primary and an adjacent secondary hue. Complementary colors are opposite hues on the color wheel, such as red and green, violet and yellow. Due to the vast range of reds, yellows, and blues, not all color wheels introduce the same primary hues (fig. **3**). Primaries are considered absolute colors and cannot be created by mixing other colors together. However, mixing the primaries into various combinations creates an infinite number of colors.

2

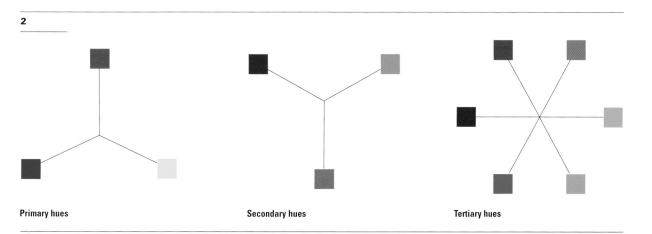

Primary hues   Secondary hues   Tertiary hues

Value

Value refers to the lightness or darkness of a color. It is a variable that can substantially alter a color's appearance, and as we will see in the next chapter, it is also an important factor in achieving legibility with type and color. A hue changes in value when either white or black are added to it. A color with added white is called a tint (fig. **4**); a color with added black is called a shade (fig. **5**). Generally speaking, pure hues that are normally light in value (yellow, orange, green) make the best tints, while pure hues that are normally dark in value (red, blue, violet) make the most desirable shades. The palette of colors below shows a spectrum of tints and shades based on the hues from the color wheel (fig. **6**). Looking at these colors clearly shows that changes in value greatly expand color possibilities. The bottom row (fig. **7**), consisting of the achromatic colors white, black, and gray, is presented in increments of 10%.

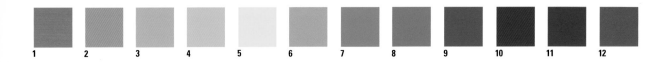

| 1 | 2 | 3 | 4 | 5 | 6 | 7 | 8 | 9 | 10 | 11 | 12 |

Twelve basic hues

_____

6

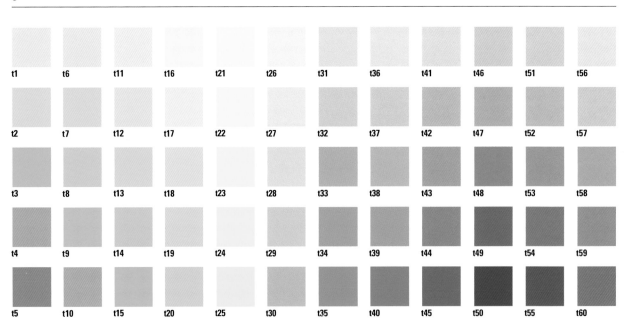

t1	t6	t11	t16	t21	t26	t31	t36	t41	t46	t51	t56
t2	t7	t12	t17	t22	t27	t32	t37	t42	t47	t52	t57
t3	t8	t13	t18	t23	t28	t33	t38	t43	t48	t53	t58
t4	t9	t14	t19	t24	t29	t34	t39	t44	t49	t54	t59
t5	t10	t15	t20	t25	t30	t35	t40	t45	t50	t55	t60

Tints

_____

4

A note about the color used in this book.
The process colors below include five tints of each pure hue on the color wheel, five shades, and the achromatic hues for a total of 143 colors. The colors are numbered for reference to the type and color combinations in chapter 4, and the case studies in chapter 5. This color palette could be expanded to include the most subtle variations, but quantity of colors is not the most important consideration. While in fact this palette offers hundreds of color possibilities, it is far more critical to learn to control color as it is used for typographic applications, and to develop a sensitive eye. When it comes to working with color and type, less is more. A CMYK conversion chart for the colors is located on page 154.

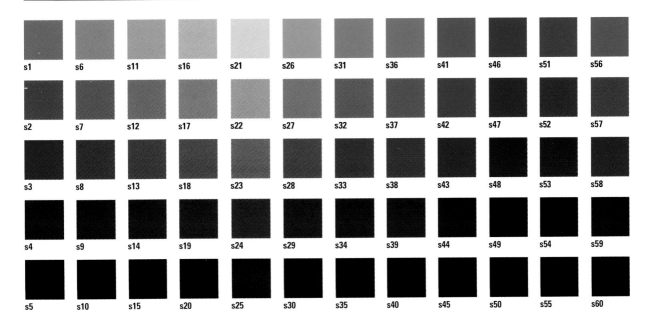

s1	s6	s11	s16	s21	s26	s31	s36	s41	s46	s51	s56
s2	s7	s12	s17	s22	s27	s32	s37	s42	s47	s52	s57
s3	s8	s13	s18	s23	s28	s33	s38	s43	s48	s53	s58
s4	s9	s14	s19	s24	s29	s34	s39	s44	s49	s54	s59
s5	s10	s15	s20	s25	s30	s35	s40	s45	s50	s55	s60

Shades

5

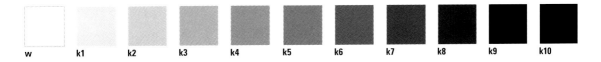

| w | k1 | k2 | k3 | k4 | k5 | k6 | k7 | k8 | k9 | k10 |

Achromatic colors

Saturation

Also called chroma or intensity, saturation refers to the brightness of a hue. The highest saturation occurs in colors that are pure and unmixed. Any color mixture will diminish intensity. However, adding white, gray, black, or a complementary color most radically compromises intensity (fig. **8**). Variations of a single hue dulled in intensity by different amounts of an added complement are often referred to as tones. When complementary colors are placed in close proximity, the intensity of each is increased. This vibrant condition is referred to as simultaneous contrast (fig. **9**).

Color temperature

The terms "warm" and "cool" are used to express those hues that connote these respective qualities. In general, reds, oranges, and yellows "feel" warm, while blues, greens, and purples "feel" cool. Distinctions between warm and cool colors can be very subtle. For example, white paper can appear either warmer or cooler depending upon the slight influence of red or blue. The same applies to gray and black (fig. **10**).

a a a a a

These five letters demonstrate the principle of color saturation. The first letter is fully saturated and is the brightest. The second letter has added black and is darker; the third letter has white added to it and is lighter; the fourth contains red, the complement of green, and is darker and duller; the fifth letter has added blue and appears duller than the fully saturated color.

8

Two fully saturated and complementary colors vibrate as a result of simultaneous contrast.

9

warm
warmer
hot

Red, orange, and yellow are colors that suggest warmth. Colors appear hotter as yellow decreases and as red increases.

cool
cooler
cold

Blue, turquoise, and green are cool colors; blue is very cold. Green is slightly warmer due to the addition of yellow.

warm gray
cool gray

Warm gray contains a small percentage of red while cool gray casts a slight blue.

10

Seeing color

Perhaps the most important concept to realize about color is that it is conditional. No single color can be judged outside of its environment. Colors physically affect one another. We owe a debt to Josef Albers, an influential artist, designer, and educator who first developed a theory based on his observations about the relativity of color. His writings have pivotally influenced artists and designers for half a century. In his book *Interaction of Color* he states, "First, it should be learned that one and the same color evokes innumerable readings." He demonstrates that the same color can appear very different when placed on different backgrounds, and that different colors can appear nearly the same when juxtaposed with different backgrounds. In addition to changes in hue, colors are influenced in terms of lightness and darkness, warmness and coolness, and brightness and dullness, depending upon surrounding colors. When working with color and type, it is important to be aware of all the ways in which color contrasts can be accomplished. Albers advocated an active, experimental approach to color, one of practice before theory. The only way to truly see and understand a color is to observe it in relationship to its environment. In this sense, color can be "read" by designers and applied with sensitivity and sound judgment. The examples on this page reveal the interdependent nature of color (fig. **11**).

The two letters to the left are identical in color. Placing them on two different backgrounds makes them appear different in both hue and value. The dark green background absorbs green from the left *a*, leaving it lighter and more yellow. Conversely, the bright yellow background absorbs yellow from the right *a*, leaving it darker and bluer.

Two identical warm red letters appear very different on different backgrounds. The warm background makes the left letter *a* appear cooler, while the cool background of the right letter *a* accentuates the letter's warmth.

Though these two letters are the same color, a light background makes the letter *a* on the left appear less bright than the letter *a* on the right, which has a dark background.

11

Color transparency

When working with color and type, it is important to establish color harmony, a condition
resulting both from the choice of colors and
their order in the visual field. Black, white, and
gray always form a harmonious relationship
because they resemble each other. Harmony is
enhanced, however, when the sequence
progresses naturally from black to gray to white
(fig. **12**). Just as artists mix paints to create new
colors, designers working with a computer can
"mix" colors by selecting mixtures from
available color palettes. Color mixing is simply
finding relationships among colors. Mixing two
colors to form a third, for example, creates a
visual bridge between the first two colors. The
third color is an offspring hue resembling both
parents. Placing a mixed color between two
parent colors is not only a harmonious ordering
of the hues, it creates the surprising illusion of
transparency. The original two colors appear as
sheets of colored acetate that overlap and form
a third color (fig. **13**). The ability to find
similarities among colors is an important part
of the color selection process, for it provides a
way of achieving harmony and concordance
among all the colors in a design.

**Black to gray to white forms
a natural and harmonious
sequence.**

12

**One is able to see just a
subtle hint of the red-violet
as the rather opaque light
yellow overlaps it.**

**A dark and light version of a
hue combine to form a
medium version of the hue.**

**The intense red is just
transparent enough to allow
the light yellow to peek
through it.**

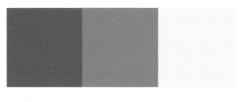

**The green appears to overlap
and darken the blue.**

13

The color triangle

The color triangle is a diagram that shows the interrelationships of hue, black, and white, and the intermediate tints, shades, and gray (fig. **14**). Selecting colors along any axis of the triangle will generally result in harmonious combinations. It is important to realize that black, white, and hue are absolute, and that tints, shades, and grays possess innumerable vari- ations. The axes shown with bold lines represent combinations that are very effective for use with type and background. Below, a few examples of the color triangle illustrate harmonious color combinations (fig. **15**).

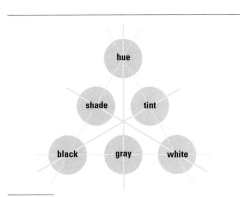

14

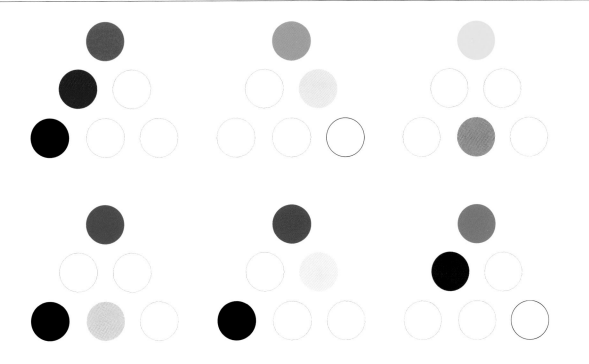

15

The basic color schemes

The color schemes below provide models for the exploration of harmonious, inventive, and communicative color combinations fig. **16**). All of these schemes are based upon the physical laws, relationships, and inherent structure of the color wheel. It is significant that these color formulations are at the heart of the chromatic displays found in nature: red desert sandstone glowing against a deep indigo sky; the variegated green perennial garden, accented with crimson blooms. The basic color schemes are at the root of most effective color combinations and may be used alone or combined into more elaborate combinations. An understanding of these schemes is essential when working with color and type, for they provide a departure point for further color investigation. When used

Primary
A combination of the primary hues, red, yellow, and blue, these colors are elemental and pure.

Secondary
Any combination of the secondary colors violet, orange, and green, and their tints and shades.

Tertiary
Any combination of the eight tertiary colors: red-orange, yellow-green, blue-violet, blue-green, yellow-orange, and red-violet. These hybrid colors fall between the primaries and secondaries on the color wheel.

Monochromatic
Consists of any single hue and its tints and shades

Achromatic
Combinations of black, white, and gray hues.

16

with type, color should always be chosen for its visual appeal as well as for its ability to communicate and promote typographic legibility. With the aid of these basic schemes, you can venture daringly into uncharted terrain to create color combinations that are both functional and emotionally charged. Color is bold, soft, energetic, somber, feminine, masculine, trendy, and traditional. A limitless

communicator, color is capable of expressing the richness of culture, or portraying something as exciting as a calypso dance or as musty as a smoky restaurant. The case studies found in chapter 5 demonstrate how the basic color schemes can be expanded and adapted in creative typographic designs.

To provide a mental picture of the relative locations of colors on the color wheel, small color wheel diagrams, such as the one pictured here, accompany the schemes on this spread and in the color combinations in chapter 4. Compare these to the actual color wheel on page 18.

Complementary
A scheme comprising any two colors and their tints and shades that are directly opposite one another on the color wheel.

Split complementary
A juxtaposition of any hue and the two colors located on either side of its complement.

Analogous
Consists of a combination of colors that are adjacent to one another on the color wheel.

Neutral
A hue combined with a percentage of its complement or black.

Incongruous
Offbeat combinations consisting of a hue and a color to the right or left of its complement.

When color and type are combined, the visual as well as the emotional attributes of type are enhanced. At the same time, changing the color of type or its background can significantly affect legibility.

Color and type

When color and type are combined, the visual as well as the emotional attributes of type are enhanced. At the same time, changing the color of type or its background can significantly affect legibility. How readable you decide type should be depends upon the intent of your message. When working with color and type, remember that the following guidelines are just that . . . *guidelines* to be tested and adapted to suit the unique needs of the typographic message.

A matter of contrast

Bodoni is a refined, crisp typeface designed in the 18th century. It is at its best when presented in black on white. The extreme thick and thin relationship of its strokes are compromised when printed in any other color combination. Compare Bodoni set in three different color combinations.

Bodoni

Bodoni

Bodoni

1

Black type on a white background is easiest to read. Notice how the gray background diminishes legibility. Reversing type to appear white on black inverts the contrast relationship, making the type less legible. Although reversing type is common practice, it is not advisable to set large amounts of text in this manner.

Black type on a white background is easiest to read. Notice how as backgrounds become darker in tone, legibility diminishes.

Black type on a white background is easiest to read. Notice how as backgrounds become darker in tone, legibility diminishes.

Black type on a white background is easiest to read. Notice how as backgrounds become darker in tone, legibility diminishes.

2

The impact of hue, value, and saturation on legibility

Legible typography possesses attributes that make it readable, and if attaining typographic readability is a priority, as most often it should be, a number of important factors must be juggled. These include the choice of typeface; type size; type weight; and letter, word, and line spacing (see chapter 1). When color is applied to type, the interplay of hue, value, and saturation must be considered.

Most typefaces are designed to be read as black letters on a white ground, and they achieve optimum legibility printed in this manner (fig. 1). There is nothing ambiguous about black and white. They are completely balanced opposites, offering exquisite contrast. When reading large amounts of type, the contrast of black on white is what readers are most accustomed to (fig. 2).

The most important thing you can do to achieve optimum legibility when working with color and type is to carefully weigh the three color properties to establish appropriate contrast between letters and their background. All colors possess a definable hue, value, and intensity by their very nature. When combining color and type, balancing these characteristics is critical.

Let us look at a couple of examples. The fully saturated, complementary colors blue and orange offer plenty of hue contrast, but when applied to type and background the edges of letterforms tend to vibrate, creating a disturbing kinetic effect that quickly numbs the eyes and tires the reader. Both of these colors possess a competing brightness, fighting for attention. If one of these hues is "softened" or "pushed back" by making it lighter or darker in value (selecting a tint or shade of the hue), the type becomes much more legible (fig. **3**). In a different example, two saturated, analogous colors such as blue and green provide sufficient contrast without a disturbing, dizzying effect. Because the green appears both lighter and brighter than the blue, there may be no need for further adjustment (fig. **4**). If analogous colors are too close to each other on the color wheel and if they do not provide enough hue or value contrast, adjustments should be made to sharpen the contrast (fig. **5**).

Type presented in the highly saturated blue and orange combination is very difficult to read. Adjusting the value of either the type or the background greatly improves legibility.

Type presented in the highly saturated blue and orange combination is very difficult to read. Adjusting the value of either the type or the background greatly improves legibility.

Type presented in the highly saturated blue and orange combination is very difficult to read. Adjusting the value of either the type or the background greatly improves legibility.

Type presented in the highly saturated blue and orange combination is very difficult to read. Adjusting the value of either the type or the background greatly improves legibility.

3

Type presented in the highly saturated blue and orange combination is very difficult to read. Adjusting the value of either the type or the background greatly improves legibility. Compare the legibility of the two top and the two bottom text blocks.

Blue and yellow-green hues seem to work well here. Even so, if the value of the yellow-green is tweaked slightly, legibility improves.

Blue and yellow-green hues seem to work well here. Even so, if the value of the yellow-green is tweaked slightly, legibility improves.

4

Blue and yellow-green hues seem to work well here. Even so, if the value of the yellow-green is tweaked slightly, legibility improves.

Red and orange, analogous colors close to each other on the color wheel, do not provide sufficient contrast for adequate legibility. Using a tint of the orange greatly improves the situation.

Red and orange, analogous colors close to each other on the color wheel, do not provide sufficient contrast for adequate legibility. Using a tint of the orange greatly improves the situation.

Red and orange, analogous colors close to each other on the color wheel, do not provide sufficient contrast for good legibility. Using a tint of the orange greatly improves the situation.

5

Of all the contrasts of color, value can be used to enhance legibility most significantly. Value contrasts effectively preserve the shapes and integrity of letters, making them more easily recognizable.

A good rule of thumb is to choose colors not directly across from one another, nor too close to one another on the color wheel. There will, of course, always be exceptions. Look for compatible colors but colors which also differ

in value and intensity. If you must use a combination of hues that for some reason do not meet legibility standards, try improving them by turning value or intensity up or down.

Typeface and color

Every typeface possesses unique qualities that should be taken into consideration when choosing color. These qualities include proportion, weight, width, presence or absence

Some typefaces are less legible than others, even when printed in black on white and with optimum sizing and spacing. This is due to differences in design. Letters with extreme proportions (heavy, light, wide, or thin) or letters with visually challenging shapes are more difficult to read when color is added. Choose color combinations that preserve the integity of such typefaces. Compare the problematic examples on the left with examples on the right that incorporate proper color adjustments.

of serifs, and eccentricities in typeface design. A very thin or narrow typeface, a peculiar or ornamental face, or a script may appear very weak and illegible if hues are too similar or if values are too close. Enough contrast must exist to preserve the fidelity of the letterforms (fig. **6**).

Typographic "color"

Black and white are neutral colors. When type is printed in black or any other color, each separate type design possesses a different tone (figs. **7, 8**). This effect is sometimes referred to as typographic "color." Creating different tones for different parts of a text is important, for it is in this way that hierarchical order and emphasis are achieved. This principle is demonstrated in the text that you are now reading; the main text appears lighter, and the subheads appear darker though both are printed in black.

Notice the differences in the "color" of these ten text blocks. Though only two actual colors are used (black and red), each block of text appears different from every other block.

Notice the differences in the "color" of these ten text blocks. Though only two actual colors are used (black and red), each block of text appears different from every other block.

Notice the differences in the "color" of these ten text blocks. Though only two actual colors are used (black and red), each block of text appears different from every other block.

Notice the differences in the "color" of these ten text blocks. Though only two actual colors are used (black and red), each block of text appears different from every other block.

Notice the differences in the "color" of these ten text blocks. Though only two actual colors are used (black and red), each block of text appears different from every other block.

Notice the differences in the "color" of these ten text blocks. Though only two actual colors are used (black and red), each block of text appears different from every other block.

Notice the differences in the "color" of these ten text blocks. Though only two actual colors are used (black and red), each block of text appears different from every other block.

Notice the differences in the "color" of these ten text blocks. Though only two actual colors are used (black and red), each block of text appears different from every other block.

NOTICE THE DIFFERENCES IN THE "COLOR" OF THESE TEN TEXT BLOCKS. THOUGH ONLY TWO ACTUAL COLORS ARE USED (BLACK AND RED). EACH BLOCK OF TEXT APPEARS DIFFERENT FROM EVERY OTHER BLOCK.

NOTICE THE DIFFERENCES IN THE "COLOR" OF THESE TEN TEXT BLOCKS. THOUGH ONLY TWO ACTUAL COLORS ARE USED (BLACK AND RED). EACH BLOCK OF TEXT APPEARS DIFFERENT FROM EVERY OTHER BLOCK.

Notice the differences in the "color" of these ten text blocks. Though only two actual colors are used (black and red), each block of text appears different in color from every other block. This effect is a visual illusion created by the proportions and shapes of the typeface designs.

color

color

color

The principle of typographic "color" is also true of larger display type. Though these three words are all printed in black, each possesses a different tone due to the unique characteristics of the individual typeface designs.

8

Type spacing and color

Letter, word, and line spacing also affect type color. Words appear lighter in tone if letters are positioned further apart (fig. **9**). Likewise, as word and line spacing increase, type appears lighter in value (fig. **10**). Paying attention to the spacing needs of type as discussed in chapter 1 can greatly improve legibility when color contrasts are marginal or when large amounts of text must be set in color (fig. **11**).

Type size and color

Small type, type that is light in weight, and delicately proportioned type with serifs suffer greatly when contrast in hue or value is insufficient (fig. **12**). As type decreases in size, color contrast must increase in strength.

As letter spacing increases, words appear lighter in tone.

color color
color color
color color

9

You can achieve the illusion of darker or lighter text blocks as you decrease or increase interline spacing. Even if you are limited to the use of one color, you can create the appearance of several colors.

You can achieve the illusion of darker or lighter text blocks as you decrease or increase interline spacing. Even if limited to the use of one color, you can create the appearance of several colors.

You can achieve the illusion of darker or lighter text blocks as you decrease or increase interline spacing. Even if limited to the use of one color, you can create the appearance of several colors.

You can achieve the illusion of darker or lighter text blocks as you decrease or increase interline spacing. Even if limited to the use of one color, you can create the appearance of several colors.

10

If you find it necessary to present large amounts of text type in color, try increasing slightly the amount of space between lines. Even an additional point of space can make a significant difference, and a reader might be encouraged to continue rather than stop.

If you find it necessary to present large amounts of text type in color, try increasing slightly the amount of space between lines. Even an additional point of space can make a significant difference, and a reader might be encouraged to continue rather than stop.

If you find it necessary to present large amounts of text type in an elaborate color setting, try increasing slightly the amount of space between lines. Even an additional point of space can make a significant difference, helping a reader to more easily find the next line while reading.

11

The smaller and more delicate the type, the more value and intensity contrast is needed to ensure adequate legibility.

The smaller and more delicate the type, the more value and intensity contrast is needed to ensure adequate legibility.

The smaller and more delicate the type, the more value and intensity contrast is needed to ensure adequate legibility.

The smaller and more delicate the type, the more value and intensity contrast is needed to ensure adequate legibility.

12

Type on busy backgrounds

Busy backgrounds or textured backgrounds compete with the legibility of type. When placing type onto or reversing type from textured backgrounds, make certain there is plenty of contrast to maintain legibility (fig. **13**). When combining type with photographs, find a quiet place within the photo that will not compromise the type, or insert the type within a separate overlapping background.

Screening type

Screening type is a way to expand color options without actually having to pay for additional colors. Screens are particularly effective for one- and two-color printing jobs. Type can be printed as a screen or reversed from a screened background. The percentage of the screen affects the legibility of the type (fig. **14**).

A background texture can interfere with the type if it is too busy, loud, and abrasive. Make a color adjustment, if necessary, to uphold the type's integrity.

A background texture can interfere with the type if it is too busy, loud, and abrasive. Make a color adjustment, if necessary, to uphold the type's integrity.

A background texture can interfere with the type if it is too busy, loud, and abrasive. Make a color adjustment, if necessary, to uphold the type's integrity.

13

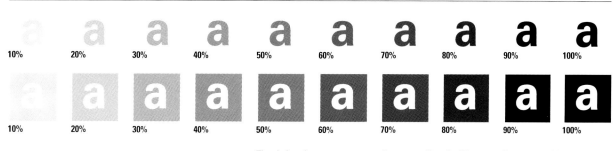

10% 20% 30% 40% 50% 60% 70% 80% 90% 100%

10% 20% 30% 40% 50% 60% 70% 80% 90% 100%

The choice of screen percentage is usually a matter of intuition. What are you trying to achieve with the type, and how legible must it be? Screens are traditionally specified in 5% increments, although computers enable you to input any percentage.

Working with process colors entails working with screens, for the wide ranging colors available for use are created with halftone dots of the process colors laid over one another (screen mixes). If type is printed in a combination of process screens – as it usually is – any inaccuracy in printing registration can result in soft, blurred, or ragged type due to straying dots. The problem is often compounded when both type and its background are printed with screen mixes. This problem is alleviated or eliminated when one or more of the process colors is 100%, when a high resolution halftone screen is used, when registration is accurate, and when type is not too small.

Type may safely be reversed from a four-color photograph to appear as white, or printed in color if there is enough contrast between the type and the photo. However, if type is too small or thin, there is an excellent chance the dots of the four-color image will invade the type characters and compromise their legibility (fig. **15**).

Outlines and shadows

If color contrast alone is not enough to make type stand out from its background, outlines and shadows can be useful. Since these treatments can be clumsy, trendy, and gimmicky, they should be used sparingly. Purpose and good judgment should guide their use. It is not advisable to use these effects with text type, for in terms of legibility they will do more harm than good. They are more successfully used with display type (fig. **16**).

A variety of outline and shadow effects.

16

Compare the placement of type in this photograph. In the left example, it is difficult to read because of the competing background. The right example shows a much more effective positioning.

15

Working with color and type on the desktop

Know about color

Before you can get the most out of working with color and type, you should become completely familiar with the basic color and type topics presented in chapters 1-3 of this book. Seek other sources as well to gain as much knowledge as you can. But reading is only the first step; confidence and competence come only through dedicated, hands-on practice.

Define your objectives

What colors to add to type is never an arbitrary decision. Know your purpose and audience, and then choose color and type combinations that best represent them. With effective combinations of color and type, you can convey the intent of the message and set just the right mood. Always make typographic legibility your primary concern, departing from it only when appropriate.

Choose color for type and background

Remember that working with color and type is always a matter of both type *and* its background. You arrive at the most legible combinations when you strive for strong contrasts of hue (warm vs. cool), value (light vs. dark), saturation (vivid vs. dull), and combinations of these. But of these contrasts, value is the most critical. Think tints and shades before hues.

Choose dark on light combinations first

Type always reads better when letters are light and backgrounds are dark. But if light type on dark backgrounds works better for your purposes, go for it. Ultimately, the most important concept to remember is that contrast in value is essential.

Strive for color harmony

Though color harmony means many things to many people, a few suggestions will provide guidance: 1) Limit the number of colors to just a few, and select one to serve as the dominant color. 2) When considering hues, choose those with common characteristics such as analogous colors, or colors opposite one another on the color wheel. Harmony can result in both similar and dissimilar colors. 3) Don't use too many vivid colors; mix it up with shades and tints of well chosen pure hues. This will also provide your design with depth. 4) Use achromatic colors with pure hues, tints, and shades, as these combinations are always harmonious. 5) Begin with the basic color schemes shown on pages 26 and 27, and elaborate upon them as necessary.

Refer to color swatchbooks

When you are working on the computer desktop and you are selecting colors that will be printed, be aware that the computer screen does not accurately represent color. Always make color selections from printed swatchbooks, and then apply these selections to elements on the screen. You will then have an accurate idea about what the chosen colors will look like on press.

Select a color library

Whether working with spot or process (cmyk) color, choose a color-matching library and use it exclusively for each design job. Each library is based on a specific color system that will aid you in achieving consistency in your color selections. Color libraries include Pantone, Toyo, Trumatch, and Focoltone.

The color properties of hue, value, and saturation are important concerns when choosing color for type and its background. Carefully balancing these three color attributes leads to legible color and type combinations.

Color and type combinations

The color properties of hue, value, and saturation are critical concerns when choosing color for type and its background. Carefully balancing these three color attributes leads to legible color and type combinations. Color is an expression of light on the computer screen, and because of its brightness and glow, it appears significantly different than ink on paper. The combinations on the following pages will aid you in making selections based upon the appearance of color and type on the printed page. These specimens will also help you to assess the relative legibility of color and type combinations and to venture into more daring and expressive color terrain. Though these specimens do not exhaust all color and type possibilities (no single source can), you will nonetheless find a practical collection based upon an interaction of hues within five basic color schemes: primary, secondary, tertiary, monochromatic, and achromatic. The color palette used is presented on pages 20 and 21. It represents a thorough range of hues, values, and saturations. Each combination is numerically keyed to the process color conversion chart on page 154 for easy reference.

Since primary colors are equidistant on the color wheel, they offer significant hue contrasts. The primaries red and blue represent color temperature extremes. An interesting by-product of warm and cool colors is that warm colors appear to advance from the background, while cool colors recede. Make note of how the red type hovers above the blue backgrounds. Altering the saturation of the blue background aids legibility; compare the legibility of *1* and *5*.

color and **type**

color and **type**

1 | type **1** background **t41**

color and **type**

color and **type**

2 | type **1** background **t42**

color and **type**

color and **type**

3 | type **1** background **t43**

color and **type**

color and **type**

4 | type **1** background **t44**

color and **type**

color and **type**

5 | type **1** background **9**

color and **type**

color and **type**

6 | type **1** background **s41**

color and **type**

color and **type**

7 | type **1** background **s42**

color and **type**

color and **type**

8 | type **1** background **s43**

color and **type**

color and **type**

9 | type **1** background **s44**

color and **type**

color and **type**

10 | type **t1** background **9**

color and **type**

color and **type**

11 | type **t2** background **9**

color and **type**

color and **type**

12 | type **t3** background **9**

color and **type**

color and **type**

13 | type **t4** background **9**

color and **type**

color and **type**

14 | type **t5** background **9**

color and **type**

color and **type**

15 | type **s1** background **9**

color and **type**

color and **type**

16 | type **s2** background **9**

color and **type**

color and **type**

17 | type **s3** background **9**

color and **type**

color and **type**

18 | type **s4** background **9**

color and type

color and **type**

19 | type **9** background **t1**

color and type

color and **type**

20 | type **9** background **t2**

color and type

color and **type**

21 | type **9** background **t3**

color and type

color and **type**

22 | type **9** background **t4**

color and type

color and type

23 | type **9** background **1**

color and type

color and type

24 | type **9** background **s1**

color and type

color and type

25 | type **9** background **s2**

color and type

color and type

26 | type **9** background **s3**

color and type

color and type

27 | type **9** background **s4**

color and type

color and **type**

28 | type **t41** background **1**

color and type

color and **type**

29 | type **t42** background **1**

color and type

color and **type**

30 | type **t43** background **1**

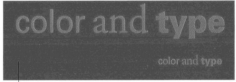

31 | type **t44** background **1**

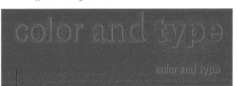

32 | type **t45** background **1**

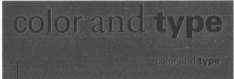

33 | type **s41** background **1**

color and type

color and **type**

34 | type **s42** background **1**

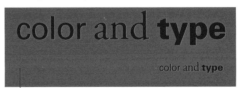

35 | type **s43** background **1**

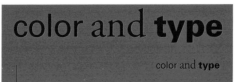

36 | type **s44** background **1**

Because they are so vivid, the hot and saturated red backgrounds engulf blue type, making it difficult to read. Legibility improves immensely with lighter red backgrounds, but these backgrounds appear more pink than red (19-22).

Yellow is the most luminous of the primary colors. Shades of yellow cast a green tint, creating the illusion of a complementary color relationship (42-45). Darker shades of red appear burgundy, and provide a contrast to the yellow backgrounds that greatly enhances legibility (51-54).

color and **type**

color and **type**

37 | type **1** background **t21**

color and **type**

color and **type**

38 | type **1** background **t22**

color and **type**

color and **type**

39 | type **1** background **t23**

color and **type**

color and **type**

40 | type **1** background **t24**

color and **type**

color and **type**

41 | type **1** background **5**

color and **type**

color and **type**

42 | type **1** background **s21**

color and **type**

color and **type**

43 | type **1** background **s22**

color and **type**

color and **type**

44 | type **1** background **s23**

color and **type**

color and **type**

45 | type **1** background **s24**

color and type

color and type

46 | type **t1** background **5**

color and type

color and type

47 | type **t2** background **5**

color and **type**

color and **type**

48 | type **t3** background **5**

color and **type**

color and **type**

49 | type **t4** background **5**

color and **type**

color and **type**

50 | type **t5** background **5**

color and **type**

color and **type**

51 | type **s1** background **5**

color and **type**

color and **type**

52 | type **s2** background **5**

color and **type**

color and **type**

53 | type **s3** background **5**

color and **type**

color and **type**

54 | type **s4** background **5**

55 type **5** background **t1**	**64** type **t21** background **1**
56 type **5** background **t2**	**65** type **t22** background **1**
57 type **5** background **t3**	**66** type **t23** background **1**
58 type **5** background **t4**	**67** type **t24** background **1**
59 type **5** background **1**	**68** type **t25** background **1**
60 type **5** background **s1**	**69** type **s21** background **1**
61 type **5** background **s2**	**70** type **s22** background **1**
62 type **5** background **s3**	**71** type **s23** background **1**
63 type **5** background **s4**	**72** type **s24** background **1**

Yellow type on a light red background appears jaundiced and difficult to read (55), while on darker shades of red, it is much more legible (60-63). The fully saturated combination of red and yellow also produces satisfying results since the two hues already differ greatly in value (59).

Primary

The inherent value contrast
of the pure hues yellow and
blue provides excellent
legibility (77). Blue type on
tints of the yellow back-
ground (73-76) and shades of
blue type on yellow back-
grounds (87-90) further
improve legibility. Darker
shades of yellow begin to
approximate the value of the
blue type, leading to a
reduction in legibility (79-81).

color and type
color and **type**
73 | type **9** background **t21**

color and type
color and **type**
74 | type **9** background **t22**

color and type
color and **type**
75 | type **9** background **t23**

color and type
color and **type**
76 | type **9** background **t24**

color and type
color and **type**
77 | type **9** background **5**

color and type
color and **type**
78 | type **9** background **s21**

color and type
color and **type**
79 | type **9** background **s22**

color and type
color and type
80 | type **9** background **s23**

81 | type **9** background **s24**

color and type
color and type
82 | type **t41** background **5**

color and type
color and **type**
83 | type **t42** background **5**

color and type
color and **type**
84 | type **t43** background **5**

color and type
color and **type**
85 | type **t44** background **5**

color and type
color and **type**
86 | type **t45** background **5**

color and type
color and **type**
87 | type **s41** background **5**

color and type
color and **type**
88 | type **s42** background **5**

color and type
color and **type**
89 | type **s43** background **5**

color and type
color and **type**
90 | type **s44** background **5**

91 | type **5** background **t41**

92 | type **5** background **t42**

93 | type **5** background **t43**

94 | type **5** background **t44**

95 | type **5** background **9**

96 | type **5** background **s41**

97 | type **5** background **s42**

98 | type **5** background **s43**

99 | type **5** background **s44**

100 | type **t21** background **9**

101 | type **t22** background **9**

102 | type **t23** background **9**

103 | type **t24** background **9**

104 | type **t25** background **9**

105 | type **s21** background **9**

106 | type **s22** background **9**

107 | type **s23** background **9**

108 | type **s24** background **9**

Placing yellow type on a blue background can be a very effective color combination, though overall, this combination is harder to read than the reverse. Yellow type on darker shades of blue (96-99) or tints of yellow on saturated blue backgrounds (100-104) provide acceptable legibility.

Because they are similar in value, the fully saturated secondary hues green and orange are not distinctive enough for a legible palette (113). Orange type on a light green background (109) appears more legible than orange type on a dark green background (117).

color and **type**

color and **type**

109 | type **3** background **t31**

color and **type**

color and **type**

110 | type **3** background **t32**

color and type

color and type

111 | type **3** background **t33**

color and **type**

color and type

112 | type **3** background **t34**

color and **type**

color and **type**

113 | type **3** background **7**

color and **type**

color and **type**

114 | type **3** background **s31**

color and **type**

color and **type**

115 | type **3** background **s32**

color and **type**

color and **type**

116 | type **3** background **s33**

color and **type**

color and **type**

117 | type **3** background **s34**

color and **type**

color and **type**

118 | type **t11** background **7**

color and **type**

color and **type**

119 | type **t12** background **7**

color and **type**

color and **type**

120 | type **t13** background **7**

color and **type**

color and **type**

121 | type **t14** background **7**

color and **type**

color and **type**

122 | type **t15** background **7**

color and **type**

color and type

123 | type **s11** background **7**

color and type

color and type

124 | type **s12** background **7**

color and **type**

color and **type**

125 | type **s13** background **7**

color and **type**

color and **type**

126 | type **s14** background **7**

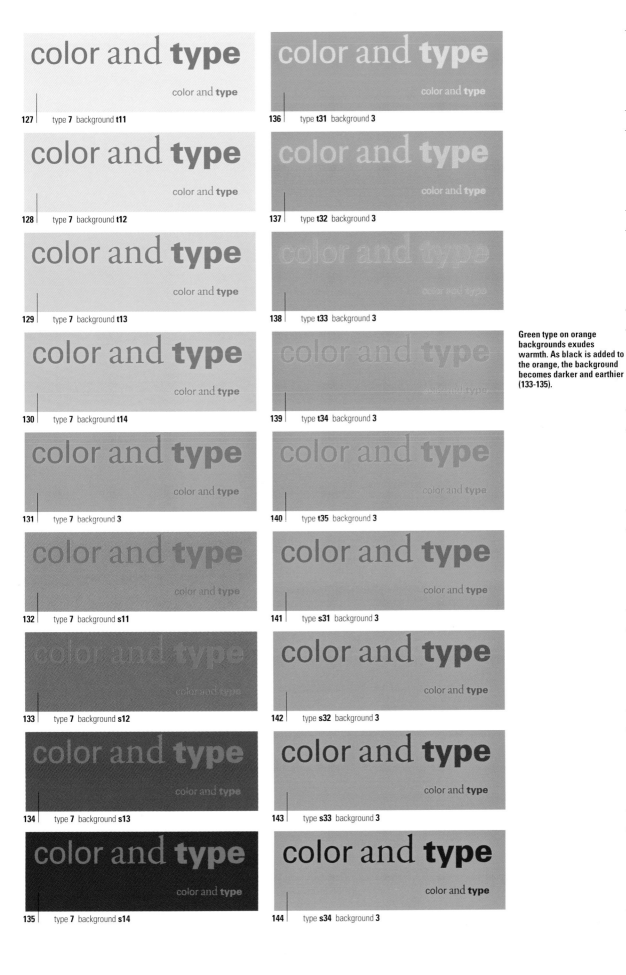

127   type **7**   background **t11**

128   type **7**   background **t12**

129   type **7**   background **t13**

130   type **7**   background **t14**

131   type **7**   background **3**

132   type **7**   background **s11**

133   type **7**   background **s12**

134   type **7**   background **s13**

135   type **7**   background **s14**

136   type **t31**   background **3**

137   type **t32**   background **3**

138   type **t33**   background **3**

139   type **t34**   background **3**

140   type **t35**   background **3**

141   type **s31**   background **3**

142   type **s32**   background **3**

143   type **s33**   background **3**

144   type **s34**   background **3**

Green type on orange backgrounds exudes warmth. As black is added to the orange, the background becomes darker and earthier (133-135).

Sufficient contrast between orange and violet translates into a readable color combination (149). As the shades of violet become darker, the orange type becomes more luminescent (150-153). The least readable combinations shown here are *147* and *162*. Violet is a regal color – pompous, sophisticated, and serious.

145   type **3**   background **t51**

146   type **3**   background **t52**

147   type **3**   background **t53**

148   type **3**   background **t54**

149   type **3**   background **11**

150   type **3**   background **s51**

151   type **3**   background **s52**

152   type **3**   background **s53**

153   type **3**   background **s54**

154   type **t11**   background **11**

155   type **t12**   background **11**

156   type **t13**   background **11**

157   type **t14**   background **11**

158   type **t15**   background **11**

159   type **s11**   background **11**

160   type **s12**   background **11**

161   type **s13**   background **11**

162   type **s14**   background **11**

163 | type **11** background **t11**

164 | type **11** background **t12**

165 | type **11** background **t13**

166 | type **11** background **t14**

167 | type **11** background **3**

168 | type **11** background **s11**

169 | type **11** background **s12**

170 | type **11** background **s13**

171 | type **11** background **s14**

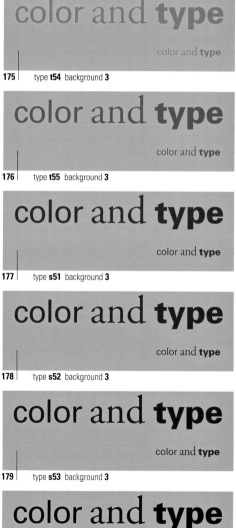

172 | type **t51** background **3**

173 | type **t52** background **3**

174 | type **t53** background **3**

175 | type **t54** background **3**

176 | type **t55** background **3**

177 | type **s51** background **3**

178 | type **s52** background **3**

179 | type **s53** background **3**

180 | type **s54** background **3**

These color combinations become less legible as the orange background grows progressively darker. *163* is the most effective combination; *171* is nearly impossible to read.

The fully saturated hues of green and violet offer enough contrast for reasonable legibility (185). Most difficult to read are *183* and *198,* where value and intensity are almost identical.

color and type

color and **type**

181 | type **7** background **t51**

color and type

color and **type**

182 | type **7** background **t52**

color and type

color and type

183 | type **7** background **t53**

color and type

color and **type**

184 | type **7** background **t54**

color and type

color and **type**

185 | type **7** background **11**

color and type

color and **type**

186 | type **7** background **s51**

color and type

color and **type**

187 | type **7** background **s52**

color and type

color and **type**

188 | type **7** background **s53**

color and type

color and **type**

189 | type **7** background **s54**

color and type

color and **type**

190 | type **t31** background **11**

color and type

color and **type**

191 | type **t32** background **11**

color and type

color and **type**

192 | type **t33** background **11**

color and type

color and **type**

193 | type **t34** background **11**

color and type

color and **type**

194 | type **t35** background **11**

color and type

color and **type**

195 | type **s31** background **11**

color and type

color and **type**

196 | type **s32** background **11**

color and type

color and type

197 | type **s33** background **11**

color and type

color and type

198 | type **s34** background **11**

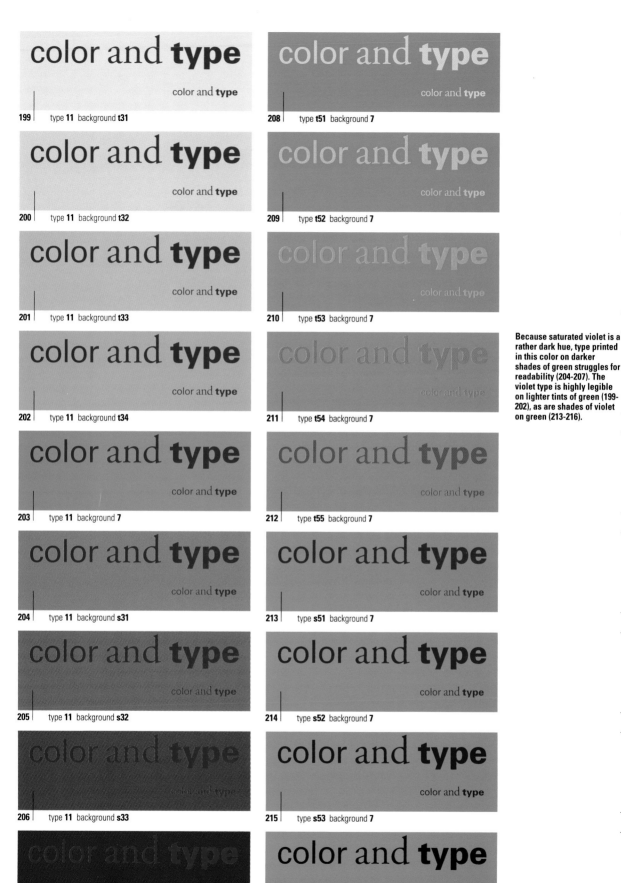

199 | type **11** background **t31**

200 | type **11** background **t32**

201 | type **11** background **t33**

202 | type **11** background **t34**

203 | type **11** background **7**

204 | type **11** background **s31**

205 | type **11** background **s32**

206 | type **11** background **s33**

207 | type **11** background **s34**

208 | type **t51** background **7**

209 | type **t52** background **7**

210 | type **t53** background **7**

211 | type **t54** background **7**

212 | type **t55** background **7**

213 | type **s51** background **7**

214 | type **s52** background **7**

215 | type **s53** background **7**

216 | type **s54** background **7**

Because saturated violet is a rather dark hue, type printed in this color on darker shades of green struggles for readability (204-207). The violet type is highly legible on lighter tints of green (199-202), as are shades of violet on green (213-216).

The two tertiary hues red-orange and yellow-orange lie close to one another on the color wheel. Since they are so similar, the most effective way to create sufficient contrast for type and background is through value. The red-orange type in full saturation reads best on lighter tints of yellow-orange (217-220); darker shades of red-orange type on yellow-orange backgrounds are also quite easy to negotiate with the eye (232-234). *223, 228, and 229* are nearly impossible to read.

color and **type**

color and **type**

217 | type **2** background **t16**

color and **type**

color and **type**

218 | type **2** background **t17**

color and **type**

color and **type**

219 | type **2** background **t18**

color and **type**

color and **type**

220 | type **2** background **t19**

color and **type**

color and **type**

221 | type **2** background **4**

color and **type**

color and **type**

222 | type **2** background **s16**

color and **type**

color and type

223 | type **2** background **s17**

color and type

color and type

224 | type **2** background **s18**

color and **type**

color and **type**

225 | type **2** background **s19**

color and **type**

color and **type**

226 | type **t6** background **4**

color and **type**

color and **type**

227 | type **t7** background **4**

color and type

color and type

228 | type **t8** background **4**

229 | type **t9** background **4**

color and **type**

color and type

230 | type **t10** background **4**

color and **type**

color and **type**

231 | type **s6** background **4**

color and **type**

color and **type**

232 | type **s7** background **4**

color and **type**

color and **type**

233 | type **s8** background **4**

color and **type**

color and **type**

234 | type **s9** background **4**

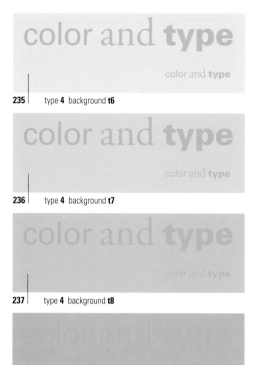

235   type **4**   background **t6**

236   type **4**   background **t7**

237   type **4**   background **t8**

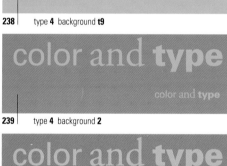

238   type **4**   background **t9**

239   type **4**   background **2**

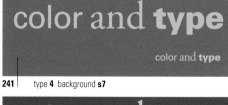

240   type **4**   background **s6**

241   type **4**   background **s7**

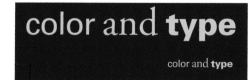

242   type **4**   background **s8**

243   type **4**   background **s9**

244   type **t16**   background **2**

245   type **t17**   background **2**

246   type **t18**   background **2**

247   type **t19**   background **2**

248   type **t20**   background **2**

249   type **s16**   background **2**

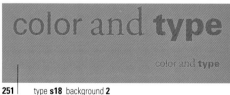

250   type **s17**   background **2**

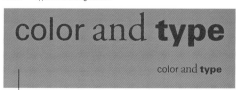

251   type **s18**   background **2**

252   type **s19**   background **2**

In reverse, this color combination lends better legibility with yellow-orange type placed on dark shades of the red-orange background (241-243), or with tints of yellow-orange type placed on red-orange backgrounds (244-246). These warm combinations are energetic and spontaneous.

Dissimilar hues are three colors apart on the color wheel. These combinations can appear quite harmonious and readable. Red-orange type on tints of yellow-green are highly readable (253-256), as are dark shades of yellow-orange type on yellow-green backgrounds (269, 270). On a somber, dark shade of yellow-green, the red-orange type reveals a glowing phosphorescence (261).

color and **type**

color and **type**

253 | type **2** background **t26**

color and **type**

color and **type**

254 | type **2** background **t27**

color and **type**

color and **type**

255 | type **2** background **t28**

color and **type**

color and **type**

256 | type **2** background **t29**

color and **type**

color and **type**

257 | type **2** background **6**

color and **type**

color and **type**

258 | type **2** background **s26**

color and **type**

color and **type**

259 | type **2** background **s27**

color and **type**

color and **type**

260 | type **2** background **s28**

color and **type**

color and **type**

261 | type **2** background **s29**

color and **type**

color and **type**

262 | type **t6** background **6**

color and **type**

color and **type**

263 | type **t7** background **6**

color and **type**

color and **type**

264 | type **t8** background **6**

color and **type**

color and **type**

265 | type **t9** background **6**

color and **type**

color and **type**

266 | type **t10** background **6**

color and **type**

color and **type**

267 | type **s6** background **6**

color and **type**

color and **type**

268 | type **s7** background **6**

color and **type**

color and **type**

269 | type **s8** background **6**

color and **type**

color and **type**

270 | type **s9** background **6**

271   type **6**   background **t6**

272   type **6**   background **t7**

273   type **6**   background **t8**

274   type **6**   background **t9**

275   type **6**   background **2**

276   type **6**   background **s6**

277   type **6**   background **s7**

278   type **6**   background **s8**

279   type **6**   background **s9**

280   type **t26**   background **2**

281   type **t27**   background **2**

282   type **t28**   background **2**

283   type **t29**   background **2**

284   type **t30**   background **2**

285   type **s26**   background **2**

286   type **s27**   background **2**

287   type **s28**   background **2**

288   type **s29**   background **2**

Placing yellow-green type on tints of red-orange is soft and tranquil (271-273). Light tints of yellow-green on red-orange prove quite legible (280-282), as well as yellow-green type on dark shades of red-orange (278-279).

Blue-green and red-orange are complementary colors, and when used at full saturation for type and background, the two colors vibrate and vie for attention (293). However, using red-orange type with turquoise (any of the lighter tints of blue-green) creates a harmonious, serene, and legible color combination (289-292). Straight red-orange type placed on darker shades of blue-green advances dynamically forward in space to create acceptable combinations (296, 297).

color and type
color and type
289 | type **2** background **t36**

color and type
color and type
290 | type **2** background **t37**

color and type
color and type
291 | type **2** background **t38**

color and type
color and type
292 | type **2** background **t39**

color and type
color and type
293 | type **2** background **8**

color and type
color and type
294 | type **2** background **s36**

color and type
color and type
295 | type **2** background **s37**

color and type
color and type
296 | type **2** background **s38**

color and type
color and type
297 | type **2** background **s39**

color and type
color and type
298 | type **t6** background **8**

color and type
color and type
299 | type **t7** background **8**

color and type
color and type
300 | type **t8** background **8**

color and type
color and type
301 | type **t9** background **8**

color and type
color and type
302 | type **t10** background **8**

color and type
color and type
303 | type **s6** background **8**

color and type
color and type
304 | type **s7** background **8**

color and type
color and type
305 | type **s8** background **8**

color and type
color and type
306 | type **s9** background **8**

color and type
color and **type**

307 | type **8** background **t6**

color and type
color and **type**

308 | type **8** background **t7**

color and type
color and **type**

309 | type **8** background **t8**

color and type
color and **type**

310 | type **8** background **t9**

color and **type**
color and **type**

311 | type **8** background **2**

color and **type**
color and **type**

312 | type **8** background **s6**

color and **type**
color and **type**

313 | type **8** background **s7**

color and **type**
color and **type**

314 | type **8** background **s8**

color and **type**
color and **type**

315 | type **8** background **s9**

color and type
color and **type**

316 | type **t36** background **2**

color and type
color and **type**

317 | type **t37** background **2**

color and type
color and type

318 | type **t38** background **2**

color and type
color and type

319 | type **t39** background **2**

color and **type**
color and **type**

320 | type **t40** background **2**

color and type
color and **type**

321 | type **s36** background **2**

color and type
color and **type**

322 | type **s37** background **2**

color and type
color and **type**

323 | type **s38** background **2**

color and type
color and **type**

324 | type **s39** background **2**

The simultaneous contrast effect (see chapter 2) is more pronounced when blue-green type is placed upon a red-orange background (311). This combination is best avoided unless you are seeking this vibrant effect. Using combinations of lighter tints and darker shades of these hues will encourage the reader to continue reading.

Red-orange and blue-violet produce a friendly, kinetic color combination. However, setting large amounts of type in this manner inhibits the reading process. Using this combination for display type can yield fresh and exciting results.

color and type
color and type

325   type **2**   background **t46**

color and type
color and type

326   type **2**   background **t47**

327   type **2**   background **t48**

color and type
color and type

328   type **2**   background **t49**

color and type
color and type

329   type **2**   background **10**

color and type
color and type

330   type **2**   background **s46**

color and type
color and type

331   type **2**   background **s47**

color and type
color and type

332   type **2**   background **s48**

color and type
color and type

333   type **2**   background **s49**

color and type
color and type

334   type **t6**   background **10**

color and type
color and type

335   type **t7**   background **10**

color and type
color and type

336   type **t8**   background **10**

color and type
color and type

337   type **t9**   background **10**

color and type
color and type

338   type **t10**   background **10**

color and type
color and type

339   type **s6**   background **10**

color and type
color and type

340   type **s7**   background **10**

color and type
color and type

341   type **s8**   background **10**

342   type **s9**   background **10**

343   type **10**   background **t6**

344   type **10**   background **t7**

345   type **10**   background **t8**

346   type **10**   background **t9**

347   type **10**   background **2**

348   type **10**   background **s6**

349   type **10**   background **s7**

350   type **10**   background **s8**

351   type **10**   background **s9**

352   type **t46**   background **2**

353   type **t47**   background **2**

354   type **t48**   background **2**

355   type **t49**   background **2**

356   type **t50**   background **2**

357   type **s46**   background **2**

358   type **s47**   background **2**

359   type **s48**   background **2**

360   type **s49**   background **2**

The simmering red-orange background is softened by the use of blue-violet for the type. Due to the relative darkness of blue-violet, legibility is compromised with the use of darker background shades of red-orange (349-351).

Neighbors on the color wheel, red-orange and red-violet have much in common. Combining them produces harmonious results, but because these hues are similar in value, it is advisable to use contrasting tints and shades. Compare the legibility of *361* with *365*.

color and **type**		color and **type**	
color and **type**		color and **type**	
361	type **2** background **t56**	370	type **t6** background **12**

color and **type**		color and **type**	
color and **type**		color and **type**	
362	type **2** background **t57**	371	type **t7** background **12**

color and **type**		color and **type**	
color and **type**		color and **type**	
363	type **2** background **t58**	372	type **t8** background **12**

color and type		color and **type**	
color and type		color and **type**	
364	type **2** background **t59**	373	type **t9** background **12**

color and **type**		color and **type**	
color and **type**		color and **type**	
365	type **2** background **12**	374	type **t10** background **12**

color and **type**		color and **type**	
color and **type**		color and type	
366	type **2** background **s56**	375	type **s6** background **12**

color and **type**		color and type	
color and **type**		color and type	
367	type **2** background **s57**	376	type **s7** background **12**

color and **type**		color and type	
color and **type**		color and type	
368	type **2** background **s58**	377	type **s8** background **12**

color and **type**		color and **type**	
color and **type**		color and **type**	
369	type **2** background **s59**	378	type **s9** background **12**

color and **type**

color and **type**

379 | type **12** background **t6**

color and **type**

color and **type**

380 | type **12** background **t7**

color and **type**

color and **type**

381 | type **12** background **t8**

color and **type**

color and **type**

382 | type **12** background **t9**

color and **type**

color and **type**

383 | type **12** background **2**

color and **type**

color and **type**

384 | type **12** background **s6**

color and **type**

color and **type**

385 | type **12** background **s7**

color and type

color and type

386 | type **12** background **s8**

color and **type**

color and **type**

387 | type **12** background **s9**

color and **type**

color and **type**

388 | type **t56** background **2**

color and **type**

color and **type**

389 | type **t57** background **2**

390 | type **t58** background **2**

391 | type **t59** background **2**

color and type

color and type

392 | type **t60** background **2**

color and **type**

color and **type**

393 | type **s56** background **2**

color and **type**

color and **type**

394 | type **s57** background **2**

color and **type**

color and **type**

395 | type **s58** background **2**

color and **type**

color and **type**

396 | type **s59** background **2**

Notice how the value of red-violet and the shade of red-orange in *385* and *391* are nearly identical. For optimum legibility, it is far better to select a background that differs more significantly in value, such as *379-381*. Of course, the appearance of a more legible color combination may not offer the desired color effect. Balancing the needs of legibility and color effect is always a challenging undertaking that necessitates careful consideration.

Yellow-orange and yellow-green are both light in value and very intense (401). It is best to combine extreme tints and shades as in *397, 405, 406,* and *414* for acceptable legibility. The yellow-green, which is accented with yellow-orange type, possesses a warmth and freshness that might remind you of a balmy summer day.

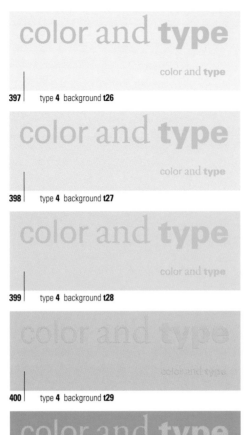

397 | type **4** background **t26**

398 | type **4** background **t27**

399 | type **4** background **t28**

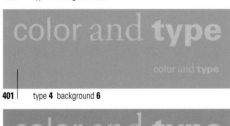

400 | type **4** background **t29**

401 | type **4** background **6**

402 | type **4** background **s26**

403 | type **4** background **s27**

404 | type **4** background **s28**

405 | type **4** background **s29**

406 | type **t16** background **6**

407 | type **t17** background **6**

408 | type **t18** background **6**

409 | type **t19** background **6**

410 | type **t20** background **6**

411 | type **s16** background **6**

412 | type **s17** background **6**

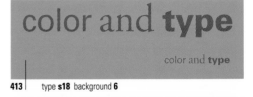

413 | type **s18** background **6**

414 | type **s19** background **6**

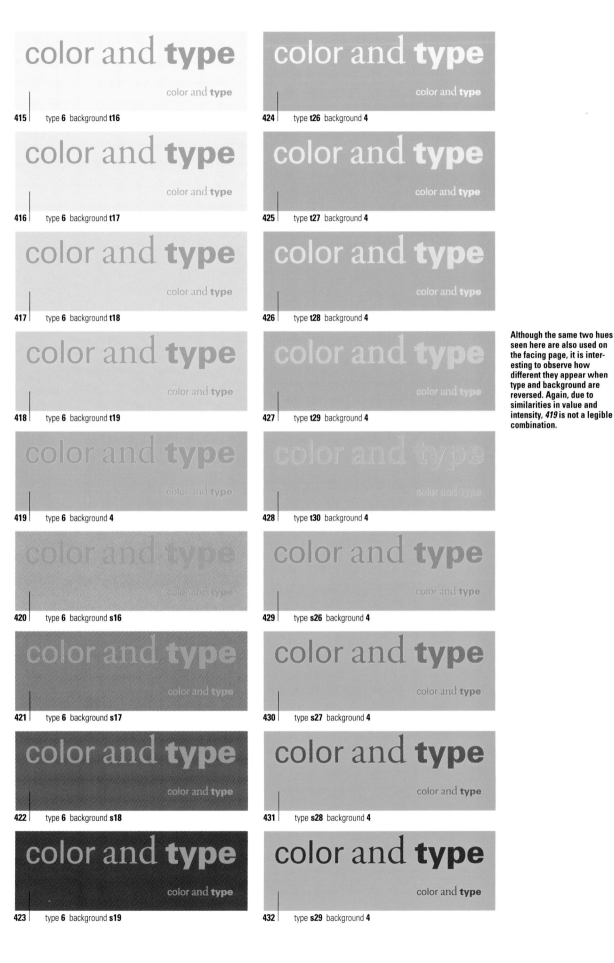

415 | type **6** background **t16**

416 | type **6** background **t17**

417 | type **6** background **t18**

418 | type **6** background **t19**

419 | type **6** background **4**

420 | type **6** background **s16**

421 | type **6** background **s17**

422 | type **6** background **s18**

423 | type **6** background **s19**

424 | type **t26** background **4**

425 | type **t27** background **4**

426 | type **t28** background **4**

427 | type **t29** background **4**

428 | type **t30** background **4**

429 | type **s26** background **4**

430 | type **s27** background **4**

431 | type **s28** background **4**

432 | type **s29** background **4**

Although the same two hues seen here are also used on the facing page, it is interesting to observe how different they appear when type and background are reversed. Again, due to similarities in value and intensity, *419* is not a legible combination.

The yellow-orange type warms the cool, aquatic blue-green and they form a harmonious color alliance. The golden hue of the type provides enough body and strength to be quite readable when placed upon lighter tints of the background (433, 434). Placed upon darker shades of the background, the type casts an elegant glow (441).

color and type
color and type

433 | type **4** background **t36**

color and type
color and type

434 | type **4** background **t37**

color and type
color and type

435 | type **4** background **t38**

color and type
color and type

436 | type **4** background **t39**

color and type
color and type

437 | type **4** background **8**

color and type
color and type

438 | type **4** background **s36**

color and type
color and type

439 | type **4** background **s37**

color and type
color and type

440 | type **4** background **s38**

color and type
color and type

441 | type **4** background **s39**

color and type
color and type

442 | type **t16** background **8**

color and type
color and type

443 | type **t17** background **8**

color and type
color and type

444 | type **t18** background **8**

color and type
color and type

445 | type **t19** background **8**

color and type
color and type

446 | type **t20** background **8**

color and type
color and type

447 | type **s16** background **8**

color and type
color and type

448 | type **s17** background **8**

color and type
color and type

449 | type **s18** background **8**

color and type
color and type

450 | type **s19** background **8**

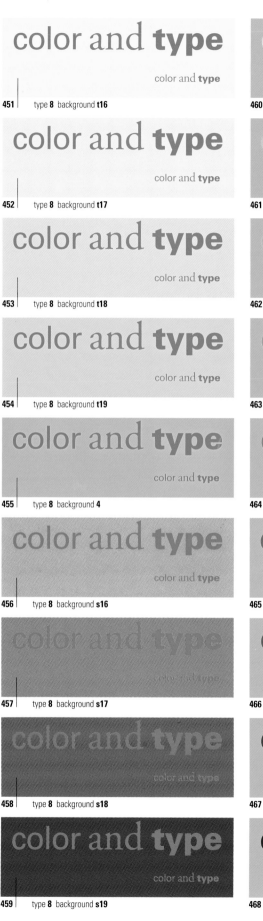

451 | type **8** background **t16**

452 | type **8** background **t17**

453 | type **8** background **t18**

454 | type **8** background **t19**

455 | type **8** background **4**

456 | type **8** background **s16**

457 | type **8** background **s17**

458 | type **8** background **s18**

459 | type **8** background **s19**

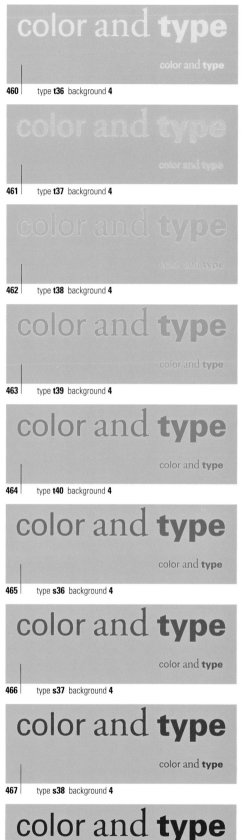

460 | type **t36** background **4**

461 | type **t37** background **4**

462 | type **t38** background **4**

463 | type **t39** background **4**

464 | type **t40** background **4**

465 | type **s36** background **4**

466 | type **s37** background **4**

467 | type **s38** background **4**

468 | type **s39** background **4**

Shades of yellow-orange are rich, warm, and earthy (458, 459). Adding blue-green type cools the palette, much as a stream brings relief to the heat of a desert. Obviously, *456, 457,462,* and *463* do not provide enough contrast between type and background for sound legibility.

This color combination, a union of the complementary colors blue-violet and yellow-orange, connotes royalty, lavishness, and pomp and ceremony. Yellow-orange type stands out best and is most easy to read on darker shades of blue-violet (474-477).

469 type **4** background **t46**	478 type **t16** background **10**
470 type **4** background **t47**	479 type **t17** background **10**
471 type **4** background **t48**	480 type **t18** background **10**
472 type **4** background **t49**	481 type **t19** background **10**
473 type **4** background **10**	482 type **20** background **10**
474 type **4** background **s46**	483 type **s16** background **10**
475 type **4** background **s47**	484 type **s17** background **10**
476 type **4** background **s48**	485 type **s18** background **10**
477 type **4** background **s49**	486 type **s19** background **10**

color and **type**

color and **type**

487 | type **10** background **t16**

color and **type**

color and **type**

488 | type **10** background **t17**

color and **type**

color and **type**

489 | type **10** background **t18**

color and **type**

color and **type**

490 | type **10** background **t19**

color and **type**

color and **type**

491 | type **10** background **4**

color and **type**

color and **type**

492 | type **10** background **s16**

color and **type**

color and **type**

493 | type **10** background **s17**

color and **type**

color and **type**

494 | type **10** background **s18**

color and **type**

color and **type**

495 | type **10** background **s19**

color and type

color and type

496 | type **t46** background **4**

color and type

color and type

497 | type **t47** background **4**

color and type

color and **type**

498 | type **t48** background **4**

color and **type**

color and **type**

499 | type **t49** background **4**

color and **type**

color and **type**

500 | type **t50** background **4**

color and **type**

color and **type**

501 | type **s46** background **4**

color and **type**

color and **type**

502 | type **s47** background **4**

color and **type**

color and **type**

503 | type **s48** background **4**

color and **type**

color and **type**

504 | type **s49** background **4**

The inverse is true when
yellow-orange type appears
on blue-violet backgrounds;
the lighter backgrounds give
definition to the blue-violet
type, which is quite dark at
full saturation (487-490).

Lavenders – the lighter tints of red-violet – are nostalgic and romantic hues. When used as a background for yellow-orange type, however, it is advantageous to use darker values of yellow-orange (not shown). Another way to maintain legibility is to use either darker values of red-violet for the background rather than lighter values (510-513), or lighter values of yellow-orange type on saturated red-violet (514-516).

color and type color and type **505** | type **4** background **t56**	color and **type** color and **type** **514** | type **t16** background **12**
color and type color and type **506** | type **4** background **t57**	color and **type** color and **type** **515** | type **t17** background **12**
color and **type** color and **type** **507** | type **4** background **t58**	color and **type** color and **type** **516** | type **t18** background **12**
color and **type** color and **type** **508** | type **4** background **t59**	color and **type** color and **type** **517** | type **t19** background **12**
color and **type** color and **type** **509** | type **4** background **12**	color and **type** color and **type** **518** | type **t20** background **12**
color and **type** color and **type** **510** | type **4** background **s56**	color and **type** color and **type** **519** | type **s16** background **12**
color and **type** color and **type** **511** | type **4** background **s57**	color and **type** color and **type** **520** | type **s17** background **12**
color and **type** color and **type** **512** | type **4** background **s58**	color and **type** color and **type** **521** | type **s18** background **12**
color and **type** color and **type** **513** | type **4** background **s59**	color and **type** color and type **522** | type **s19** background **12**

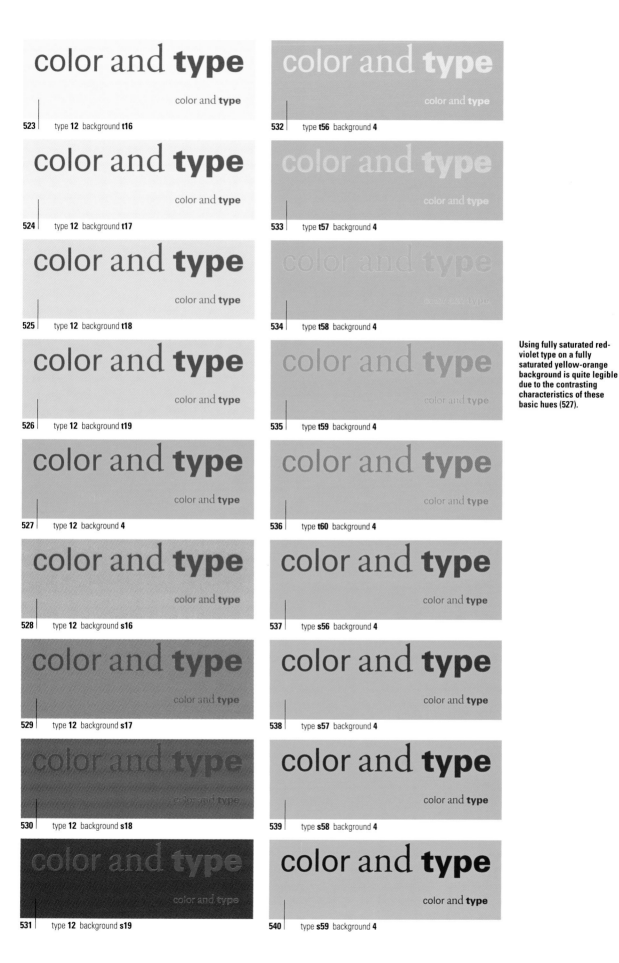

523   type **12** background **t16**

524   type **12** background **t17**

525   type **12** background **t18**

526   type **12** background **t19**

527   type **12** background **4**

528   type **12** background **s16**

529   type **12** background **s17**

530   type **12** background **s18**

531   type **12** background **s19**

532   type **t56** background **4**

533   type **t57** background **4**

534   type **t58** background **4**

535   type **t59** background **4**

536   type **t60** background **4**

537   type **s56** background **4**

538   type **s57** background **4**

539   type **s58** background **4**

540   type **s59** background **4**

Using fully saturated red-violet type on a fully saturated yellow-orange background is quite legible due to the contrasting characteristics of these basic hues (527).

This analogous combination is mellow, cool, and refreshing. Compare *549, 550,* and *558,* which are acceptably legible, with the marginally legible *544, 555,* and *556.*

color and type

color and **type**

541 type **6** background **t36**

color and type

color and **type**

542 type **6** background **t37**

color and type

color and **type**

543 type **6** background **t38**

color and type

color and type

544 type **6** background **t39**

color and type

color and **type**

545 type **6** background **8**

color and type

color and **type**

546 type **6** background **s36**

color and type

color and **type**

547 type **6** background **s37**

color and type

color and **type**

548 type **6** background **s38**

color and type

color and **type**

549 type **6** background **s39**

color and type

color and **type**

550 type **t26** background **8**

color and type

color and **type**

551 type **t27** background **8**

color and type

color and **type**

552 type **t28** background **8**

color and type

color and **type**

553 type **t29** background **8**

color and type

color and **type**

554 type **t30** background **8**

color and type

color and **type**

555 type **s26** background **8**

color and type

color and type

556 type **s27** background **8**

color and type

color and type

557 type **s28** background **8**

color and type

color and **type**

558 type **s29** background **8**

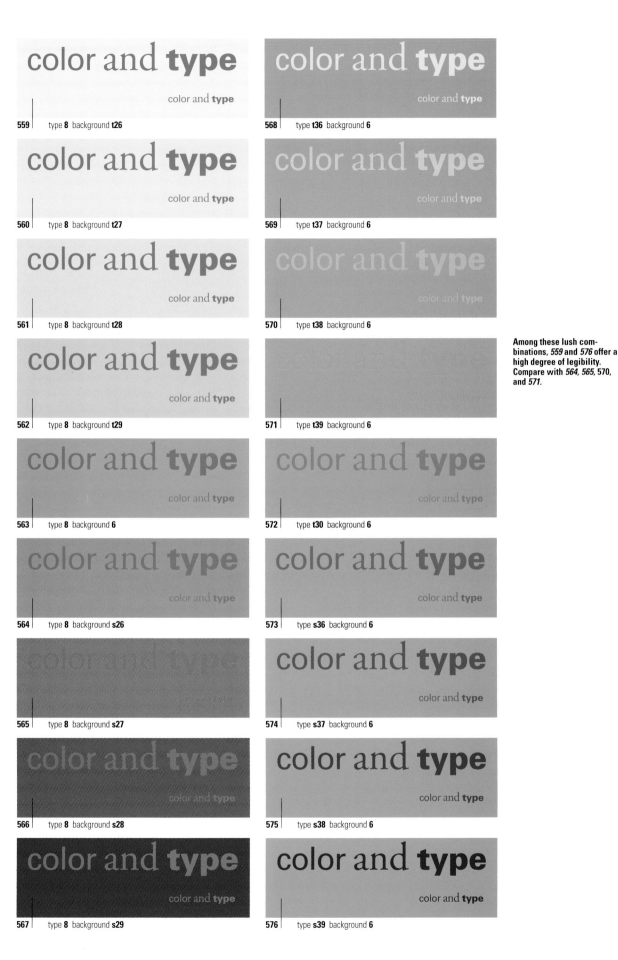

559   type **8**   background **t26**

560   type **8**   background **t27**

561   type **8**   background **t28**

562   type **8**   background **t29**

563   type **8**   background **6**

564   type **8**   background **s26**

565   type **8**   background **s27**

566   type **8**   background **s28**

567   type **8**   background **s29**

568   type **t36**   background **6**

569   type **t37**   background **6**

570   type **t38**   background **6**

571   type **t39**   background **6**

572   type **t30**   background **6**

573   type **s36**   background **6**

574   type **s37**   background **6**

575   type **s38**   background **6**

576   type **s39**   background **6**

Among these lush combinations, *559* and *576* offer a high degree of legibility. Compare with *564, 565,* 570, and *571.*

It is interesting to note the wide variety of color effects that can be achieved with colors belonging to the same families of hue. Variations in value and saturation make this possible. Compare, for example, the startling differences between *577, 581,* and *585.* While the type's hue remains constant, a shift in the value and saturation of the backgrounds gives each a unique appearance.

color and type
color and type

577 | type **6** background **t46**

color and type
color and type

578 | type **6** background **t47**

color and type
color and type

579 | type **6** background **t48**

color and type
color and type

580 | type **6** background **t49**

color and type
color and type

581 | type **6** background **10**

color and type
color and type

582 | type **6** background **s46**

color and type
color and type

583 | type **6** background **s47**

color and type
color and type

584 | type **6** background **s48**

color and type
color and type

585 | type **6** background **s49**

color and type
color and type

586 | type **t26** background **10**

color and type
color and type

587 | type **t27** background **10**

color and type
color and type

588 | type **t28** background **10**

color and type
color and type

589 | type **t29** background **10**

color and type
color and type

590 | type **t30** background **10**

color and type
color and type

591 | type **s26** background **10**

color and type
color and type

592 | type **s27** background **10**

color and type
color and type

593 | type **s28** background **10**

color and type
color and type

594 | type **s29** background **10**

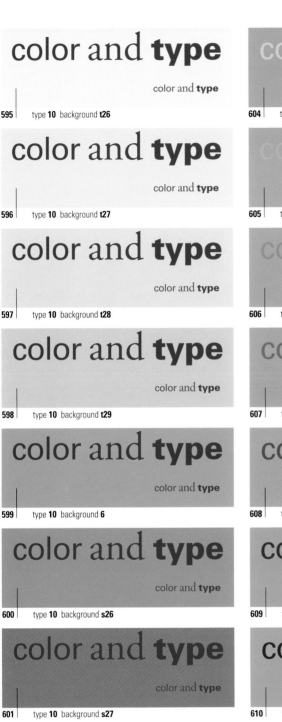

595 | type **10** background **t26**

596 | type **10** background **t27**

597 | type **10** background **t28**

598 | type **10** background **t29**

599 | type **10** background **6**

600 | type **10** background **s26**

601 | type **10** background **s27**

602 | type **10** background **s28**

603 | type **10** background **s29**

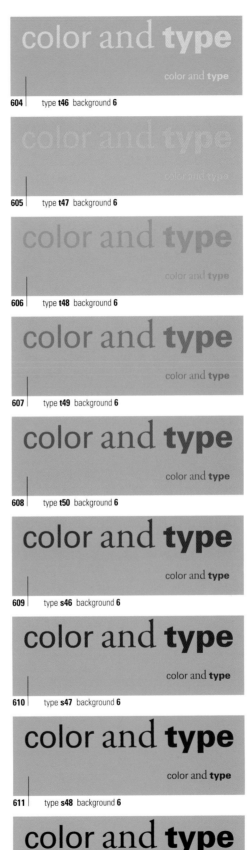

604 | type **t46** background **6**

605 | type **t47** background **6**

606 | type **t48** background **6**

607 | type **t49** background **6**

608 | type **t50** background **6**

609 | type **s46** background **6**

610 | type **s47** background **6**

611 | type **s48** background **6**

612 | type **s49** background **6**

Adequate value and saturation contrast such as in *597* makes it possible to distinguish the shapes of the letters and the spaces between them (counter-forms). When such definition and contrast are at a minimum, such as in *605*, legibility breaks down.

Combinations of the complementary hues red-violet and yellow-green are slightly off beat and whimsical. Darker shades of red-violet acquire an air of mystery and magic (620, 621).

color and type
color and type
613 | type **6** background **t56**

color and type
color and type
614 | type **6** background **t57**

color and type
color and type
615 | type **6** background **t58**

color and type
color and type
616 | type **6** background **t59**

color and type
color and type
617 | type **6** background **12**

color and type
color and type
618 | type **6** background **s56**

color and type
color and type
619 | type **6** background **s57**

color and type
color and type
620 | type **6** background **s58**

color and type
color and type
621 | type **6** background **s59**

color and type
color and type
622 | type **t26** background **12**

color and type
color and type
623 | type **t27** background **12**

color and type
color and type
624 | type **t28** background **12**

color and type
color and type
625 | type **t29** background **12**

color and type
color and type
626 | type **t30** background **12**

color and type
color and type
627 | type **s26** background **12**

color and type
color and type
628 | type **s27** background **12**

color and type
color and type
629 | type **s28** background **12**

color and type
color and type
630 | type **s29** background **12**

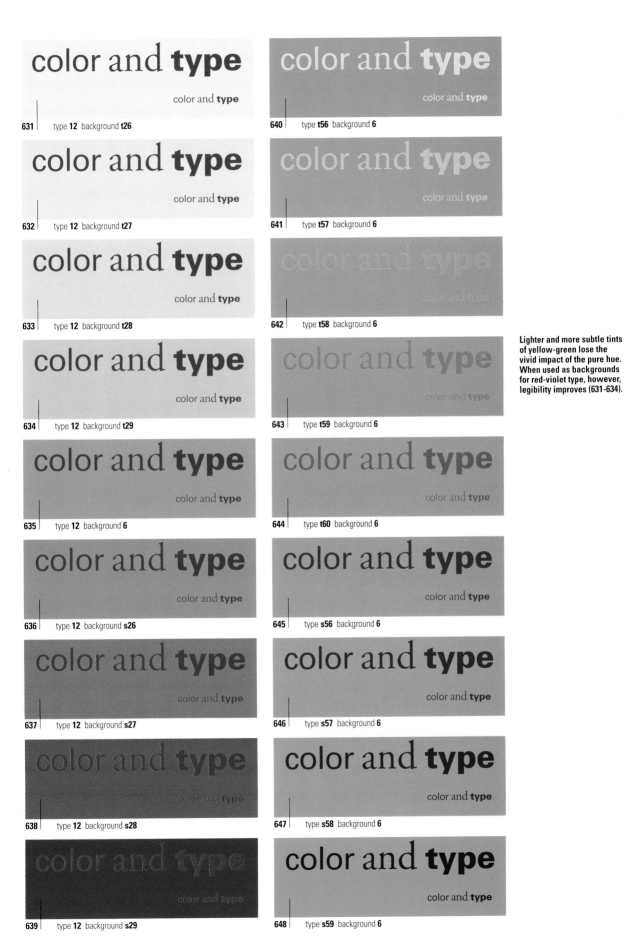

color and type
color and **type**

631 | type **12** background **t26**

color and type
color and **type**

640 | type **t56** background **6**

color and type
color and **type**

632 | type **12** background **t27**

color and **type**
color and **type**

641 | type **t57** background **6**

color and **type**
color and **type**

633 | type **12** background **t28**

color and type
color and type

642 | type **t58** background **6**

color and **type**
color and **type**

634 | type **12** background **t29**

color and type
color and type

643 | type **t59** background **6**

color and **type**
color and **type**

635 | type **12** background **6**

color and type
color and **type**

644 | type **t60** background **6**

color and **type**
color and **type**

636 | type **12** background **s26**

color and **type**
color and **type**

645 | type **s56** background **6**

color and **type**
color and **type**

637 | type **12** background **s27**

color and **type**
color and **type**

646 | type **s57** background **6**

color and **type**
color and type

638 | type **12** background **s28**

color and **type**
color and **type**

647 | type **s58** background **6**

color and type
color and type

639 | type **12** background **s29**

color and **type**
color and **type**

648 | type **s59** background **6**

Lighter and more subtle tints of yellow-green lose the vivid impact of the pure hue. When used as backgrounds for red-violet type, however, legibility improves (631-634).

In partnership, blue-green and blue-violet appear calm and restful. These analogous hues remind us perhaps of a peaceful and tranquil sea. Plenty of value contrast is needed to ensure legibility when these colors are used for type and background. Compare *658* and *666*.

color and **type**

color and **type**

649   type **8** background **t46**

color and **type**

color and **type**

650   type **8** background **t47**

color and **type**

color and **type**

651   type **8** background **t48**

color and **type**

color and **type**

652   type **8** background **t49**

color and **type**

color and **type**

653   type **8** background **10**

color and **type**

color and **type**

654   type **8** background **s46**

color and **type**

color and **type**

655   type **8** background **s47**

color and **type**

color and **type**

656   type **8** background **s48**

color and **type**

color and **type**

657   type **8** background **s49**

color and **type**

color and **type**

658   type **t36** background **10**

color and **type**

color and **type**

659   type **t37** background **10**

color and **type**

color and **type**

660   type **t38** background **10**

color and **type**

color and **type**

661   type **t39** background **10**

color and **type**

color and **type**

662   type **t40** background **10**

color and **type**

color and **type**

663   type **s36** background **10**

color and **type**

color and **type**

664   type **s37** background **10**

color and **type**

color and **type**

665   type **s38** background **10**

color and **type**

color and **type**

666   type **s39** background **10**

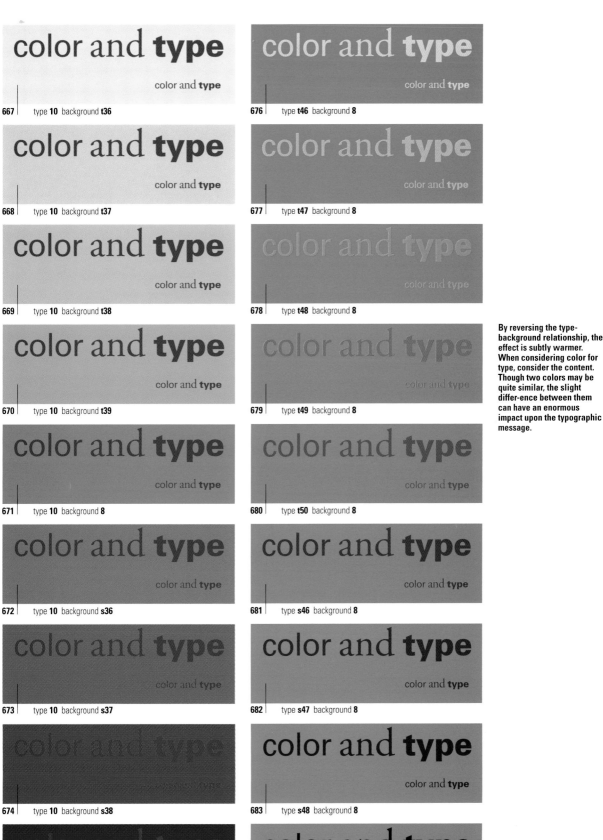

color and type

color and **type**

667   type **10**   background **t36**

color and type

color and **type**

668   type **10**   background **t37**

color and type

color and **type**

669   type **10**   background **t38**

color and type

color and **type**

670   type **10**   background **t39**

color and type

color and **type**

671   type **10**   background **8**

color and type

color and **type**

672   type **10**   background **s36**

color and type

color and **type**

673   type **10**   background **s37**

color and type

color and type

674   type **10**   background **s38**

color and type

color and type

675   type **10**   background **s39**

color and type

color and **type**

676   type **t46**   background **8**

color and type

color and **type**

677   type **t47**   background **8**

color and type

color and type

678   type **t48**   background **8**

color and type

color and type

679   type **t49**   background **8**

color and type

color and **type**

680   type **t50**   background **8**

color and **type**

color and **type**

681   type **s46**   background **8**

color and **type**

color and **type**

682   type **s47**   background **8**

color and **type**

color and **type**

683   type **s48**   background **8**

color and **type**

color and **type**

684   type **s49**   background **8**

By reversing the type-background relationship, the effect is subtly warmer. When considering color for type, consider the content. Though two colors may be quite similar, the slight differ-ence between them can have an enormous impact upon the typographic message.

Color temperature affects the relationship between these two hues in a most subtle way, for red-violet leans towards red and the warm side of the color wheel. Approaching green on the color wheel, blue-green is cool. Color temperature distinctions, regardless of their subtlety, are important to keep in mind when choosing colors.

color and type
color and type
685 | type **8** background **t56**

color and type
color and type
686 | type **8** background **t57**

color and type
color and type
687 | type **8** background **t58**

color and type
color and type
688 | type **8** background **t59**

color and type
color and type
689 | type **8** background **12**

color and type
color and type
690 | type **8** background **s56**

color and type
color and type
691 | type **8** background **s57**

color and type
color and type
692 | type **8** background **s58**

color and type
color and type
693 | type **8** background **s59**

color and type
color and type
694 | type **t36** background **12**

color and type
color and type
695 | type **t37** background **12**

color and type
color and type
696 | type **t38** background **12**

color and type
color and type
697 | type **t39** background **12**

color and type
color and type
698 | type **t40** background **12**

color and type
color and type
699 | type **s36** background **12**

color and type
color and type
700 | type **s37** background **12**

color and type
color and type
701 | type **s38** background **12**

color and type
color and type
702 | type **s39** background **12**

color and **type**

color and **type**

703   type **12** background **t36**

color and **type**

color and **type**

704   type **12** background **t37**

color and **type**

color and **type**

705   type **12** background **t38**

color and **type**

color and **type**

706   type **12** background **t39**

color and **type**

color and **type**

707   type **12** background **8**

color and **type**

color and **type**

708   type **12** background **s36**

color and type

color and type

709   type **12** background **s37**

color and type

color and type

710   type **12** background **s38**

color and **type**

color and **type**

711   type **12** background **s39**

color and **type**

color and **type**

712   type **t56** background **8**

color and **type**

color and **type**

713   type **t57** background **8**

color and type

color and type

714   type **t58** background **8**

color and type

color and type

715   type **t59** background **8**

color and type

color and type

716   type **t60** background **8**

color and **type**

color and **type**

717   type **s56** background **8**

color and **type**

color and **type**

718   type **s57** background **8**

color and **type**

color and **type**

719   type **s58** background **8**

color and **type**

color and **type**

720   type **s59** background **8**

703-706 and *717-720* are the most legible as well as the safest combinations shown here. However, *711* offers a more dramatic possibility that might be appropriate for use with display type. Compare the legibility of the display type and the text type in this combination. When a color combination might be marginal, try enlarging the type for better results.

Blue-violet and red-violet are cousins on the color wheel, and they possess extraordinary richness. Fully saturated hues, such as *725,* are always more vivid than tints and shades. When white is added, such as in the background tints of *721- 724,* the hues become softer and more pastelle in appearance.

color and type

color and type

721 | type **10** background **t56**

color and type

color and type

722 | type **10** background **t57**

color and type

color and type

723 | type **10** background **t58**

color and type

color and type

724 | type **10** background **t59**

725 | type **10** background **12**

726 | type **10** background **s56**

727 | type **10** background **s57**

728 | type **10** background **s58**

729 | type **10** background **s59**

color and type

color and type

730 | type **t46** background **12**

color and type

color and type

731 | type **t47** background **12**

color and type

color and type

732 | type **t48** background **12**

733 | type **t49** background **12**

734 | type **t50** background **12**

color and type

color and type

735 | type **s46** background **12**

color and type

color and type

736 | type **s47** background **12**

color and type

color and type

737 | type **s48** background **12**

color and type

color and type

738 | type **s49** background **12**

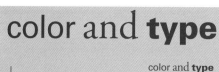

739   type **12** background **t46**

740   type **12** background **t47**

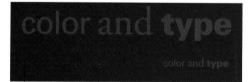

741   type **12** background **t48**

742   type **12** background **t49**

743   type **12** background **10**

744   type **12** background **s46**

745   type **12** background **s47**

746   type **12** background **s48**

747   type **12** background **s49**

748   type **t56** background **10**

749   type **t57** background **10**

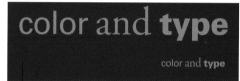

750   type **t58** background **10**

751   type **t59** background **10**

752   type **t60** background **10**

753   type **s56** background **10**

754   type **s57** background **10**

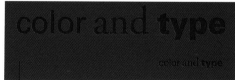

755   type **s58** background **10**

756   type **s59** background **10**

A color becomes duller as black or its complement is added to it (compare the type in *753-756*). If you wish to tone down vivid type, try adding black. If the type's background is dark, you may have to lighten it to preserve legibility.

When the same hue is used for both type and background, the only way to establish contrast is through value. As type and background approach the same value, legibility diminishes. Compare *757* with *761*.

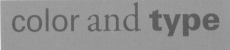

color and **type**

color and **type**

757 | type **1** background **t1**

color and **type**

color and **type**

758 | type **1** background **t2**

color and **type**

color and **type**

759 | type **1** background **t3**

color and **type**

color and **type**

760 | type **1** background **t4**

color and **type**

color and **type**

761 | type **1** background **t5**

color and **type**

color and **type**

762 | type **1** background **s1**

color and **type**

color and **type**

763 | type **1** background **s2**

color and **type**

color and **type**

764 | type **1** background **s3**

color and **type**

color and **type**

765 | type **1** background **s4**

color and **type**

color and **type**

766 | type **t1** background **1**

color and **type**

color and **type**

767 | type **t2** background **1**

color and **type**

color and **type**

768 | type **t3** background **1**

color and **type**

color and **type**

769 | type **t4** background **1**

color and **type**

color and **type**

770 | type **t5** background **1**

color and **type**

color and **type**

771 | type **s1** background **1**

color and **type**

color and **type**

772 | type **s2** background **1**

color and **type**

color and **type**

773 | type **s3** background **1**

color and **type**

color and **type**

774 | type **s4** background **1**

color and **type**

color and **type**

775 | type **9** background **t41**

color and **type**

color and **type**

784 | type **t41** background **9**

color and **type**

color and **type**

776 | type **9** background **t42**

color and **type**

color and **type**

785 | type **t42** background **9**

color and **type**

color and **type**

777 | type **9** background **t43**

color and **type**

color and **type**

786 | type **t43** background **9**

color and **type**

color and **type**

778 | type **9** background **t44**

color and **type**

color and **type**

787 | type **t44** background **9**

color and type

color and type

779 | type **9** background **t45**

color and type

color and type

788 | type **t45** background **9**

color and type

color and type

780 | type **9** background **s41**

color and type

color and type

789 | type **s41** background **9**

color and type

color and type

781 | type **9** background **s42**

color and **type**

color and **type**

790 | type **s42** background **9**

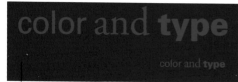

color and type

color and type

782 | type **9** background **s43**

color and **type**

color and **type**

791 | type **s43** background **9**

color and **type**

color and **type**

783 | type **9** background **s44**

color and **type**

color and **type**

792 | type **s44** background **9**

Even though you may be limited to the use of a single color, you can achieve a great deal of chromatic variety by juxtaposing different values of the color.

When working with type, the achromatic colors black, white, and gray are extremely useful. Because of their absolute neutrality, they are highly versatile. This is a no-nonsense palette: resolute, serious, and businesslike.

color and type
color and type

793 | type **k10** background **k1**

color and type
color and type

794 | type **k10** background **k2**

color and type
color and type

795 | type **k10** background **k3**

color and type
color and type

796 | type **k10** background **k4**

color and type
color and type

797 | type **k10** background **k5**

color and type
color and type

798 | type **k10** background **k6**

color and type
color and type

799 | type **k10** background **k7**

color and type
color and type

800 | type **k10** background **k8**

801 | type **k10** background **k9**

color and type
color and type

802 | type **k1** background **k10**

color and type
color and type

803 | type **k2** background **k10**

color and type
color and type

804 | type **k3** background **k10**

color and type
color and type

805 | type **k4** background **k10**

color and type
color and type

806 | type **k5** background **k10**

color and type
color and type

807 | type **k6** background **k10**

color and type
color and type

808 | type **k7** background **k10**

color and type
color and type

809 | type **k8** background **k10**

810 | type **k9** background **k10**

811   type **w**   background **k1**

820   type **k1**   background **w**

color and type
color and **type**

812   type **w**   background **k2**

color and **type**
color and **type**

821   type **k2**   background **w**

color and type
color and **type**

813   type **w**   background **k3**

color and **type**
color and **type**

822   type **k3**   background **w**

color and type
color and **type**

814   type **w**   background **k4**

color and **type**
color and **type**

823   type **k4**   background **w**

Grays, which can be created from screen tints of black, are customarily presented in 10% increments. Progressing from 10% to 90% black, type becomes increasingly more legible (820-828). Solid black type proves most legible.

color and type
color and **type**

815   type **w**   background **k5**

color and **type**
color and **type**

824   type **k5**   background **w**

color and type
color and **type**

816   type **w**   background **k6**

color and **type**
color and **type**

825   type **k6**   background **w**

color and type
color and **type**

817   type **w**   background **k7**

color and **type**
color and **type**

826   type **k7**   background **w**

color and type
color and **type**

818   type **w**   background **k8**

color and **type**
color and **type**

827   type **k8**   background **w**

color and type
color and **type**

819   type **w**   background **k9**

color and **type**
color and **type**

828   type **k9**   background **w**

The next six pages display type in the 12 basic hues of the color wheel on white, gray, and black backgrounds. You will find that each hue responds differently to the achromatic palette and that legibility differs enormously depending upon the value and intensity of each hue. Legibility is at its worst when the values of the background and the type become too similar. For example, the red type in *834* approximates the gray background, leading to a decrease in legibility.

color and **type**

color and **type**

829 | type **1** background **w**

color and **type**

color and **type**

830 | type **1** background **k2**

color and **type**

color and **type**

831 | type **1** background **k3**

color and **type**

color and **type**

832 | type **1** background **k4**

color and **type**

color and **type**

833 | type **1** background **k5**

color and **type**

color and **type**

834 | type **1** background **k6**

color and **type**

color and **type**

835 | type **1** background **k7**

color and **type**

color and **type**

836 | type **1** background **k8**

color and **type**

color and **type**

837 | type **1** background **k10**

color and **type**

color and **type**

838 | type **2** background **w**

color and **type**

color and **type**

839 | type **2** background **k2**

color and **type**

color and **type**

840 | type **2** background **k3**

color and **type**

color and **type**

841 | type **2** background **k4**

color and **type**

color and **type**

842 | type **2** background **k5**

color and **type**

color and **type**

843 | type **2** background **k6**

color and **type**

color and **type**

844 | type **2** background **k7**

color and **type**

color and **type**

845 | type **2** background **k8**

color and **type**

color and **type**

846 | type **2** background **k10**

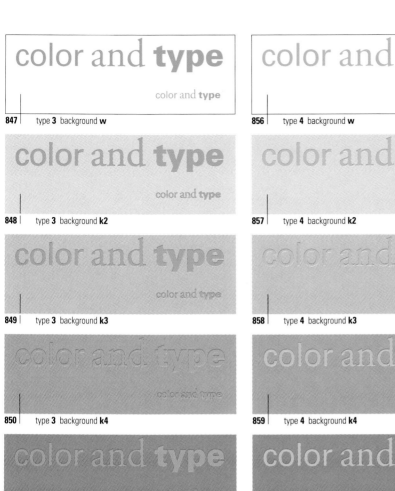

847 | type **3** background **w**

856 | type **4** background **w**

848 | type **3** background **k2**

857 | type **4** background **k2**

849 | type **3** background **k3**

858 | type **4** background **k3**

850 | type **3** background **k4**

859 | type **4** background **k4**

Regardless of which hue is combined with white, black, or gray, the result is almost always harmonious and beautiful. The achromatic hues enhance the chromatic hues, never competing with their essential qualities.

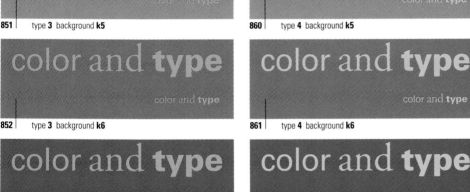

851 | type **3** background **k5**

860 | type **4** background **k5**

852 | type **3** background **k6**

861 | type **4** background **k6**

853 | type **3** background **k7**

862 | type **4** background **k7**

854 | type **3** background **k8**

863 | type **4** background **k8**

855 | type **3** background **k10**

864 | type **4** background **k10**

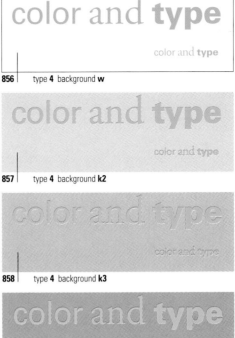

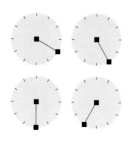

On a white background, yellow type lacks definition (865). As backgrounds grow darker, type becomes more vivid (866-872). Too much contrast can also affect legibility. On black, for example, yellow type creates a dazzle that can tire a reader if used for large quantities of text type (873).

color and **type**

color and **type**

865 | type **5** background **w**

color and **type**

color and **type**

874 | type **6** background **w**

color and type

color and type

866 | type **5** background **k2**

color and **type**

color and **type**

875 | type **6** background **k2**

color and **type**

color and type

867 | type **5** background **k3**

color and **type**

color and **type**

876 | type **6** background **k3**

color and **type**

color and **type**

868 | type **5** background **k4**

color and **type**

color and type

877 | type **6** background **k4**

color and **type**

color and **type**

869 | type **5** background **k5**

color and **type**

color and type

878 | type **6** background **k5**

color and **type**

color and **type**

870 | type **5** background **k6**

color and **type**

color and type

879 | type **6** background **k6**

color and **type**

color and **type**

871 | type **5** background **k7**

color and **type**

color and type

880 | type **6** background **k7**

color and **type**

color and **type**

872 | type **5** background **k8**

color and **type**

color and type

881 | type **6** background **k8**

color and **type**

color and **type**

873 | type **5** background **k10**

color and **type**

color and **type**

882 | type **6** background **k10**

color and **type**   color and **type**

color and **type**   color and **type**

883 | type **7** background **w**   892 | type **8** background **w**

color and **type**   color and **type**

color and **type**   color and **type**

884 | type **7** background **k2**   893 | type **8** background **k2**

color and **type**   color and **type**

color and **type**   color and **type**

885 | type **7** background **k3**   894 | type **8** background **k3**

color and **type**   color and **type**

color and **type**   color and **type**

886 | type **7** background **k4**   895 | type **8** background **k4**

color and **type**   color and **type**

color and **type**   color and **type**

887 | type **7** background **k5**   896 | type **8** background **k5**

color and type   color and type

color and type   color and type

888 | type **7** background **k6**   897 | type **8** background **k6**

color and type   color and type

color and type   color and type

889 | type **7** background **k7**   898 | type **8** background **k7**

color and **type**   color and **type**

color and **type**   color and **type**

890 | type **7** background **k8**   899 | type **8** background **k8**

color and **type**   color and **type**

color and **type**   color and **type**

891 | type **7** background **k10**   900 | type **8** background **k10**

Type in each hue appears to change colors as it interacts differently with each achromatic background. Notice how the green and blue-green type nearly disappears on the 50% gray background (887, 896).

Blue type is peaceful and soothing on gray. It reads best on white and the lighter shades of gray (901-904). Legibility suffers on the darker shades of gray and black (905-909). This is generally true of all of the darker hues.

color and **type**
color and **type**

901 | type **9** background **w**

color and **type**
color and **type**

902 | type **9** background **k2**

color and **type**
color and **type**

903 | type **9** background **k3**

color and **type**
color and **type**

904 | type **9** background **k4**

color and **type**
color and **type**

905 | type **9** background **k5**

color and **type**
color and **type**

906 | type **9** background **k6**

color and **type**
color and **type**

907 | type **9** background **k7**

color and **type**
color and **type**

908 | type **9** background **k8**

color and **type**
color and **type**

909 | type **9** background **k10**

color and **type**
color and **type**

910 | type **10** background **w**

color and **type**
color and **type**

911 | type **10** background **k2**

color and **type**
color and **type**

912 | type **10** background **k3**

color and **type**
color and **type**

913 | type **10** background **k4**

color and **type**
color and **type**

914 | type **10** background **k5**

color and **type**
color and **type**

915 | type **10** background **k6**

color and **type**
color and **type**

916 | type **10** background **k7**

color and **type**
color and **type**

917 | type **10** background **k8**

color and **type**
color and **type**

918 | type **10** background **k10**

color and **type**

color and **type**

919   type **11**   background **w**

color and **type**

color and **type**

928   type **12**   background **w**

color and **type**

color and **type**

920   type **11**   background **k2**

color and **type**

color and **type**

929   type **12**   background **k2**

color and **type**

color and **type**

921   type **11**   background **k3**

color and **type**

color and **type**

930   type **12**   background **k3**

color and **type**

color and **type**

922   type **11**   background **k4**

color and **type**

color and **type**

931   type **12**   background **k4**

color and **type**

color and **type**

923   type **11**   background **k5**

color and **type**

color and **type**

932   type **12**   background **k5**

color and **type**

color and **type**

924   type **11**   background **k6**

color and **type**

color and **type**

933   type **12**   background **k6**

color and **type**

color and **type**

925   type **11**   background **k7**

color and **type**

color and type

934   type **12**   background **k7**

color and **type**

color and **type**

926   type **11**   background **k8**

color and type

color and type

935   type **12**   background **k8**

color and type

color and type

927   type **11**   background **k10**

color and **type**

color and **type**

936   type **12**   background **k10**

Because white reflects more light than any other color, it is generally an effective background choice for type. The intrinsic properties of any hue are best preserved when paired with white.

Observing how others solve the mysteries of color and type can be informative as well as inspiring, and it can open doors to new and exciting possibilities in your own work.

Observing how others solve the mysteries of color and type can be instructional as well as inspiring, and it can open doors to new and exciting possibilities in your own work. Everyone possesses different color sensibilities and opinions, and a color scheme that works for one person is not necessarily acceptable to another. No formula or single "right" answer to any color and type problem exists. Subsequently, you have to make decisions based upon the timeless principle of *appropriateness*. This is to say that the solution to a problem should always arise from within the problem and not outside of it. The following 30 case studies represent a wide range of printed applications and reveal how top designers address the problems of color and type. You will find helpful tips throughout that will shed light on your own work.

Borrowing from the collection of colors on pages 20 and 21, color swatches on the left-hand pages provide an approximation of the colors used in the examples, as well as the quantity and relative location of the colors within the design. The purpose of these color swatches is to illustrate the general properties of the colors used in the projects. No attempt is made to exactly duplicate the color schemes. These color combinations are keyed to the color conversion chart on page 154 for reference.

Design:
Jack Anderson
Heidi Favour
Mary Hermes
Mary Chin Hutchison
Julia LaPine
Hornall Anderson Design Works, Inc.
Art Direction:
Jack Anderson

TIP: Just as important as the specific colors chosen for a design, the extent (quantity) of the colors and their proximity to each other are equally critical. Take advantage of the computer's ability to readily test many possibilities.

When the Print NW/Six Sigma company changed its name to Quebecor Integrated Media, they had an announcement designed to inform the public of the change. The announcement depicts three logos, each printed in black on vivid panels of both primary and secondary colors. Words describing the capabilities of the company are printed in a subtle, tinted varnish and extend across the entire announcement. This technique provides the piece with visual depth. The same colors are used for stationery and other items, bringing unity to the entire program.

1

The chosen values of the colors ensure that black type remains readable when printed on top. Compare the varying levels of legibility of black type when printed on different values of a background color.

color and type	color and type
color and type	color and type
color and type	color and type

3

Stationery and binders are printed in the same palette of colors for a unified look.

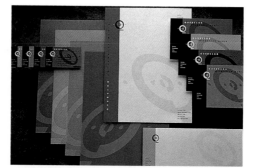

2

The secondary colors of green, orange, and violet blend effectively with a primary blue to produce a pleasing collection of hues. The effect of the colors is striking, communicating energy and vision. The physical position of the colors in the announcement is very important for the overall effect. This example illustrates how the color effect changes as the position of hues is altered.

k10

t59

t45

4

t30

Typeface: Futura

On the back side of the announcement, the colors are repeated to reveal the company's name, *Quebecor Integrated Media.* The intensity of the color and the small lines of type are heightened by the solid black background.

Quebecor: Turning Technology Into Solutions.

1.800.451.5742

Your single source for Media delivery services.

An Integrated network of manufacturing facil...

Design:
Bob Dinetz
Art Direction:
Bill Cahan
Cahan & Associates

Color harmony can be achieved by juxtaposing analogous colors as demonstrated by the dominant use of the yellow, light yellow, and green in this publication. Accenting these hues with opposite colors on the color wheel adds to visual stimulation.

T I P :

Trident Microsystems designs, develops, and markets multimedia video processing chipsets, GUI accelerators, and graphics controllers. The annual report presented here communicates the company's achievements in this technology and in the marketplace. An animated message imitating a video screen changes from *FOLLOW* to *LEAD* as the reader shifts the cover from one position to another. The technologies that position the company for success are featured inside the annual report through an array of video images and an intensely bright palette of colors.

1

The word *LEAD* is repeated again on the first page of the report to reiterate the company's position as a leader. The word consists of orange letters with red outlines, a technique that creates emphasis and visual prominence.

LEAD

2

The three elements of the company's success – capabilities, relationships, and design – are presented in three interior spreads. A detail from one of these spreads shows a unique use of color and type. Appearing on top of a video image, the numeral *3* appears in three variations. These include the *3* with a black shadow, a red outline, and outlined in white. These numerals are stacked on top of one another but offset slightly for an energetic and vibrating appearance.

3

The letter to stockholders uses color to emphasize key information. Heads appear in black type of a bold weight, while highlighted information appears in red. The rest of the letter is printed in black type of a regular weight.

LETTER TO   *STOCKHOLDERS*

4

For financial charts, yellow ruled lines offer a subtle but effective alternative to commonly used black ruled lines.

exercitable and vest cumulatively in 25% increments upon the anniversary of the date of grant.

The following table summarizes the option activities for the years ended June 30, 1992, 1994 and 1995.

(IN THOUSANDS, EXCEPT PER SHARE DATA)	OPTIONS AVAILABLE FOR GRANT	OPTIONS OUTSTANDING NUMBER OF OPTIONS	PRICE PER OPTION
Balance, June 30, 1992	307	692	$0.77–$ 5.00
Additional shares reserved	1,300	—	
Options granted	(841)	841	$5.00–$17.00
Options exercised	—	(76)	$0.77–$ 5.00
Options expired or canceled	189	(189)	$0.77–$ 7.00
Balance, June 30, 1993	955	1,256	$0.77–$17.00
Options granted	(1,606)	1,665	$4.63–$ 7.30
Options exercised	—	(107)	$0.77–$ 6.00
Options expired or canceled	803	(860)	$1.05–$16.75
Balance, June 30, 1994	150	1,864	$0.77–$ 7.00
Additional shares reserved	800	—	
Options granted	(1,008)	1,008	$1.55–$20.06
Options exercised	—	(231)	$0.80–$ 6.00
Options expired or canceled	335	(335)	$0.80–$16.75
Balance, June 30, 1995	277	2,316	$0.77–$20.06

At June 30, 1995, 1994 and 1993, options for 691,000, $19,000 and 276,000 shares of Common Stock were vested but not exercised. In July 1993, the Company canceled 830,000 options outstanding under the Option Plan with exercise prices

t42
9
1
t23
6
5

Typefaces: Din Schriften, Univers

The cover, printed in a
dazzlingly saturated yellow,
cannot be ignored. This color
combined with the
lead/follow message entices
the reader into the pages of
the annual report.

CAPABILITIES

etail taken from the jack-
eveals the subtle trans-
nt effect created by
rlapping transparent inks.
rs become darker and
e neutral at the point of
rsection.

A detail from the flap of the
book's jacket reveals a
single block of text type
printed over three different
background colors. The
pastel text, appearing to float
delicately above the surface
of the paper, is darker or
lighter in value depending on
which of the colors it
overlaps.

The only annual devoted exclusively to typographic
design, Typography 16 presents the finest work in this
field from 1994. Selected from 2,894 international
submissions to the forty-first Type Directors Club
competition (TDC41), the 239 winning designs are
models of excellence and innovation in contemporary
type design.

This year's selection encompasses a wide range of
categories, among them posters, logotypes, packaging,
promotions, books, stationery, magazines, television
graphics, annual reports, videos, and corporate
identities. Entries are displayed in full color and are
accompanied by informative captions listing the
designer, client, typography, and more.

The Judge's Choice section features the winning
entries from the year's competition that have been
singled out by each of the seven judges as his or her

The typographic forms found
on the cover are reintro-
duced in a new variation on
the title spread.

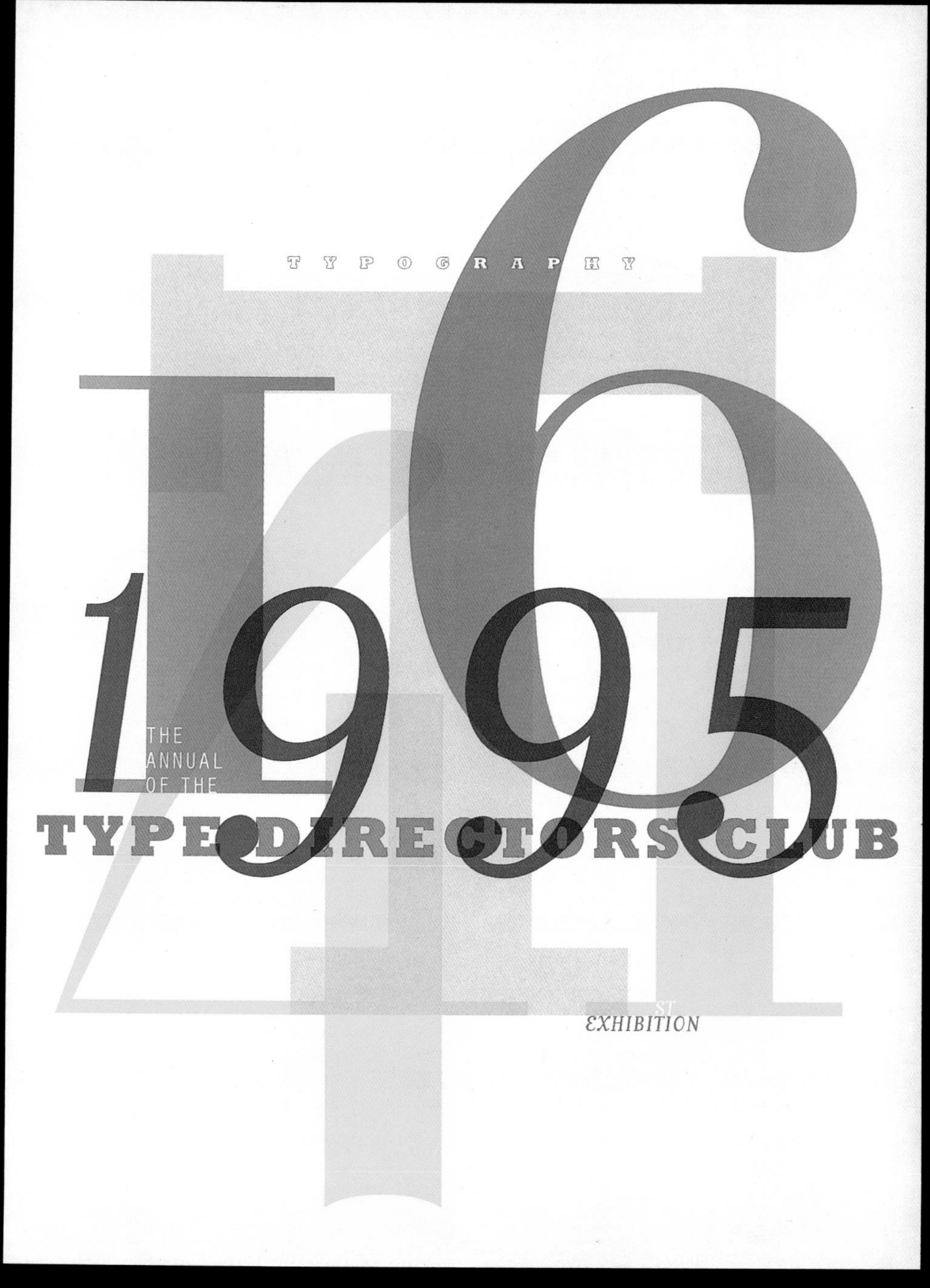

TYPOGRAPHY

16

1995

THE
ANNUAL
OF THE

TYPE DIRECTORS CLUB

41ST

EXHIBITION

The typography on the jacket is simultaneously chaotic and orderly, a blend of intentions that raises the reader's curiosity. While the letterforms are precisely arranged, sized, and aligned, their overlap creates a complex maze, a varied garden of shape and color through which the eye wanders.

Design:
Scott Allison

TIP: Primary colors are the purest of hues; they cannot be formed by any other combination of colors. Use them when your design calls for a pure, elemental, and straightforward tone.

Piet Mondrian was an abstract painter whose theories about color and space were the basis of an art and design movement called de Stijl – an important movement that originated in Holland in 1917. Mondrian's paintings were reduced to straight lines, squares, rectangles, and the colors red, yellow, green, blue, black, white, and gray. This booklet, which features the work of Mondrian, explores and emulates the visual vocabulary of the artist.

1

On the cover, alternating primary hues suggest the color cadence of a Mondrian painting. Title typography possesses a similar rhythmic structure.

p i e t
m o n d r i a n
p a i n t   a n d   p r o c e s s

2

A detail from the contents page reveals a playground of type and color. Words are transformed into an intriguing visual pattern by the strategic insertion of red and yellow letters. We are reminded of the careful articulation of Mondrian's own forms.

c o n t e n t s

1	youth + education
2	process
3	abstraction
4	time line
5	maturity
6	bibliography
7	colophon

3

In a detail from a timeline within the booklet, words assigned primary colors emphasize the content.

1 9 4 0 — 4 4   continues to develop paintings; compositions reach an unrivaled intensity in composition of line, plane, and color

w
k10
k7
9
5
1

Typefaces: Helvetica, Serifa

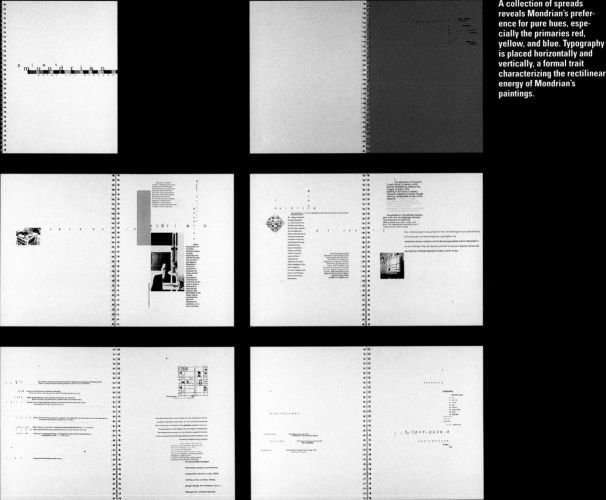

A collection of spreads reveals Mondrian's preference for pure hues, especially the primaries red, yellow, and blue. Typography is placed horizontally and vertically, a formal trait characterizing the rectilinear energy of Mondrian's paintings.

ARTNOW is a series of exhibitions sponsored by the Montgomery Museum of Fine Arts. Brochures are designed to tie events together as a series and to provide a consistent visual look. Design elements for the brochures include an identifying logotype used for the series title, a vertical bar containing the name of the featured artist, and a four-color reproduction of the artist's work. Colors for each brochure reflect those used by the artist. This approach not only helps to distinguish each of the brochures, it also informs the reader about the specific color palettes.

TIP: Place type and images on black backgrounds if you wish to create visual drama. Most any color harmonizes with black.

1

The red *T* in the *ARTNOW* logotype emulates the red in the cover painting. The color also provides the mark with visual distinction and makes the word *ART* more readable. Compare the logotype with and without the red *T*.

2

While only a hint of red exists on the cover, a full-bleed sea of the hue on the back cover dazzles the reader. Compare the white headline and caption on the back cover to the rest of the text, which is set in black. A heightened contrast between the white letters and the red background projects these elements forward in space, giving them hierarchical prominence.

3

In the process of determining which colors should be used for the logotype, several combinations were tested. A few of the possibilities are exhibited here. The version with a red *T* was chosen for its visual impact.

t43

1

k10

Typefaces: Franklin Gothic, Helvetica

A vertical bar containing the artist's name casts the same hue as in the painting. Extracting color from the cover painting and applying it to various typographic elements provides visual unity. Simultaneously, the juxtaposition of hot red and cool blue hues provides a resonant contrast.

When type and photographs containing light hues are placed upon black backgrounds – as in this cover – the entire space glows.

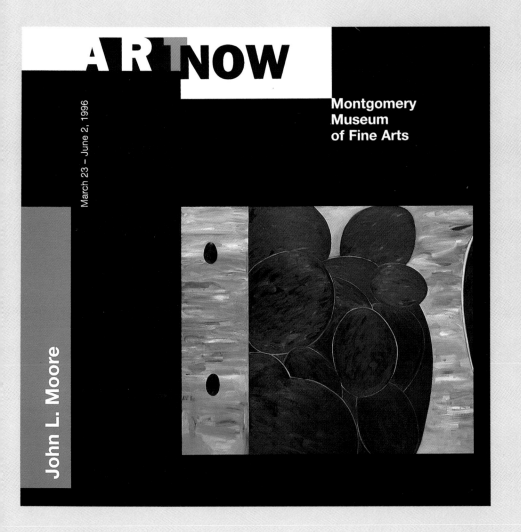

ART NOW

Montgomery
Museum
of Fine Arts

March 23 – June 2, 1996

John L. Moore

Design:
Jack Anderson
David Bates
Mary Hermes
John Anicker
Mary Chin Hutchison
Hornall Anderson Design Works, Inc.
Art Direction:
Jack Anderson
Illustration:
Yutaka Sasaki
Photography:
Tom Collicott

TIP: To emphasize elements such as words and phrases within text, try using colors that contrast with the main body of the text. For more emphasis use stronger contrast and for less emphasis use weaker contrast.

NEXTLINK specializes in the next wave of telecommunications services, focusing specifically upon local phone service customers who desire telecommunications reliability and up-to-date technology. Distinctive typography, custom lettering, and bold colors provide the company with a visual identity program that projects a highly progressive image. The company operates flexibly. . . one foot in the future.

1

The logotype suggests the futuristic outlook of the company. A gradation beginning with red-violet and ending with yellow-orange travels through the space age letters of NEXTLINK. The letter *X* – a metaphor for a communications link – casts a shadow as it rises into new technological realms. Unlike the rest of the letters of the logotype, the *X* is carved from a curved plane of rainbow color.

2

The *X* is most dramatic as it appears on the cover. Diecut through each page of the brochure, it forms a window from front to back. As the brochure is held to light, the *X* glows brilliantly. The background is silent and black, a deep space through which the *X* travels.

3

Within the brochure, black text type is punctuated with yellow-orange call-outs that stress important points.

4

The style and weight of text type reversed from photographs help to maintain legibility.

Typefaces: Eagle Book, Gill Sans

Each spread of the brochure contains a photograph casting a specific tertiary hue. The X whose background reflects the hues contained within the photographs is on the right-hand page, adjacent the photographs.

T I P :

When appropriate, get as much mileage from two colors as possible by combining them in different ways. Use solid colors, reverse type to appear as white, and screen tints of the colors in different combinations.

The purpose of this three-fold brochure is to demonstrate the capabilities of Dupli-graphic as a high-quality, two-color printer. Colors used for the brochure are a primary metallic blue (the corporate color) and black. Ink is applied to only one side of a translucent sheet, and when folded, the type and images peer through to the other side as well. A smiling woman wearing sun glasses encourages the reader to "take a look" at the capabilities of the printer. Together, the type, images, color, translucent paper, and folds create an intriguing and mirror-like message.

1
As demonstrated by the typographic configuration on the inside of the brochure, a tremendous variety of type and color effects is possible using only two colors. Here we see type printed in two different solid colors, reversed from these colors to appear as white, and printed with screen mixes of the two colors to create a variety of tones.

2
When reversing type from solid color backgrounds, a number of factors affect legibility. Among these is the weight of type. Letter strokes, serifs, and punctuation of overly light type can appear too light; the counters (spaces within letters, such as in the lowercase e) of letters in heavy type may appear too small for adequate letter definition. Aggravating this problem is the printing phenomenon known as ink squeeze, where ink oozes over the edges of letter strokes and further thins them. Generally, medium weight type is most legible when reversed from solid color backgrounds. Compare the legibility of light, medium, and bold type reversed from identical color backgrounds.

color and type

color and type

color and type

3
Creating outline and solid rectangular shapes in each of the two colors to enclose type blocks contributes to the variety of the brochure.

s43

k10

Typefaces: Akzidenz Grotesk, Akzidenz Grotesk Extended

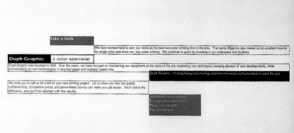

The colors gradually grow in intensity as the gate-folded brochure is unfolded. Only when it is completely unfolded are the colors viewed at full strength. The cover features the woman showing through from the opposite side of the sheet (top). Unfolding the brochure for the first time reveals a composite image: a very faint image of the woman as she peeks through from beneath the folded panel; a numeral 2; and two spots of blue aligned with the lenses of the sunglasses (middle). The unfolded brochure reveals all of the parts (bottom).

When you are limited to using black as your only color, don't think of it as a limitation. By using a full spectrum of tones (from white to black), you can achieve lively and harmonious results.

TIP:

Black and white and the achromatic grays can appear amazingly colorful when light and dark values are effectively utilized. Similar to walking in a winter garden, the bright colors of summer yield to subtle hues playing upon faded foliage. The LinoGraphics Capabilities brochure is printed entirely in black ink on translucent paper. Type and images converse through layers of pages for a highly textured and tactile reading experience.

1

Remarkable variety can be achieved in type by using screens of black in different combinations. Note the stimulating, shimmering effect of these variations. Typographic legibility depends upon the amount of value contrast incorporated into each combination.

color and type   color and type   color and type

color and type   color and type   color and type

color and type   color and type   color and type

color and type   color and type   color and type

color and type   color and type   color and type

2

For a chart on the last page of the brochure, black type, white type on black and gray backgrounds, overlapping type, and type with generous letter spacing combine to create an active, vibrant texture.

3

Outlined type, graphic icons, ruled lines, and photographs mingle in harmony and contribute to the brochure's appeal.

k10

Typeface: Imago

The cover and inside cover reveal how type and images printed on both sides of the sheet can be viewed simultaneously. As viewed from the front, black elements printed on the opposite side appear gray, creating a rich tonality and a separation of elements.

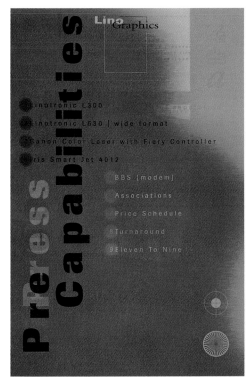

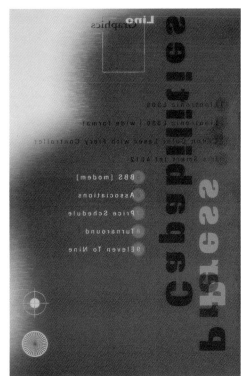

A selection of spreads from the brochure reveals a rich blend of black and white and grays. Despite the apparent complexity of the pages, type and images remain readable due to a careful orchestration of color values. At the same time, serendipity guides the interaction of color and type.

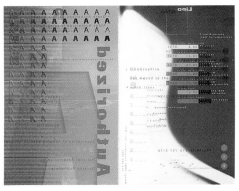

Art Direction:
Dana Lytle
Kevin Wade
Planet Design Co.

TIP: Triadic colors are separated by three other colors on the color wheel. As demonstrated by this catalog which utilizes triadic colors, you can use these hues to create both contrast and color harmony. Triadic colors are hues that differ from one another but also share common characteristics.

The intent of this retail catalog is to convey the elegance and style associated with the Saris products, which are roof rack systems for bicycles, skis, canoes, and other recreational equipment. The type is playful to allude to the sports of cycling, skiing, and paddling, but it also reflects the technical aspects of precision storage rack systems. The color palette consists of primary and secondary hues and is both sophisticated and funky.

1

Each page of the Saris catalog features a different background color. These are presented as circular blends that "spotlight" the products from page to page. For this catalog only one color was needed for the circular blends, but it is possible to combine different colors for a variety of effects.

2

At the tops of pages, running heads consisting of type on black bars make it easy for the reader to navigate the catalog. The type is printed in the same color as the background, creating the dimensional effect that it is cut away from the black bar to expose the underlying background.

hitch racks
Saris

3

On the back cover, an animated phrase is printed in both black and the yellow-green background color. Because the yellow-green letters appear over light areas of the same color blend, they remain readable; however, they are very subtle, receding quietly into space.

k10
s21
4
t39
s22
t44

Typeface: Letter Gothic

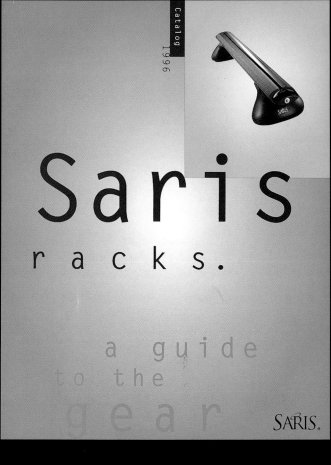

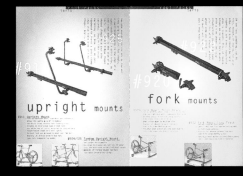

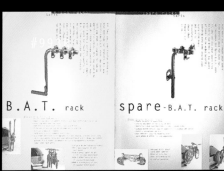

Each page of the catalog is a kinetic and rather complex organization of elements. Product images and type appear in constant motion, swirling about one another in space. Despite the seeming randomness of the pages, the size and color of the type elements and images establish a clear hierarchy. Product information appears as light gray patches of text type, while product names appear in large, black type. Product numbers, also large in size, are printed in white for immediate recognition.

Design:
Clifford Stoltze
Tracy Schroder
Heather Kramer
Peter Farrell
Resa Blatman
Stoltze Design

TIP: Don't be timid about taking daring chances with color and type. In this way you can discover color combinations that stand out and make an unforgettable statement. Do be sure, however, to select color that is appropriate to the needs of the design problem.

Through design and color, the Massachusetts College of Art catalog emulates a highly charged and experimental learning environment. Both primary and secondary hues present images and type, and they are shifted in value and saturation for a most unusual palette.

Flipping through the pages reveals an intriguing kaleidoscope of shapes, colors, and typographic treatments. Never a dull moment, the catalog parts with convention yet remains accessible and informative.

1
Consisting of black and hot, red type, the title thrusts forward from the background, which is a photographic montage with a muted yellow cast. The catalog's spine is blue. A detail of the cover shows the distribution of the title colors. Appearing in red, *MASS ART* is separated from *Massachusetts College of Art* to reveal the abbreviated pronunciation of the college's name.

2
Many risks are taken with color and type that defy legibility standards, but given the experimental nature of the institution, this is quite acceptable. The left example shows small, yellow-green text type printed over a red photograph. Though not easy to read, with effort the type is nonetheless readable. The context of a message and the intended audience are always important aspects to consider before testing the limits of typographic legibility. For the most part, the youthful audience of this catalog will have little trouble reading this text. The right example is a more normative page containing information that the reader must easily access.

3
In this detail we see how color and type are manipulated into a visual metaphor. The word *students* presents a kaleidoscope of colors, referring to the word *kaleidoscopic.*

4
Part of the charm of this publication is the tapestry of overlapping and layered type, color, and images.

k10
s22
2
t45

112 113

Typefaces: Calvino, Scala

Representative spreads
display a wild, exuberant
collection of colors, textures,
shapes, and letterforms.

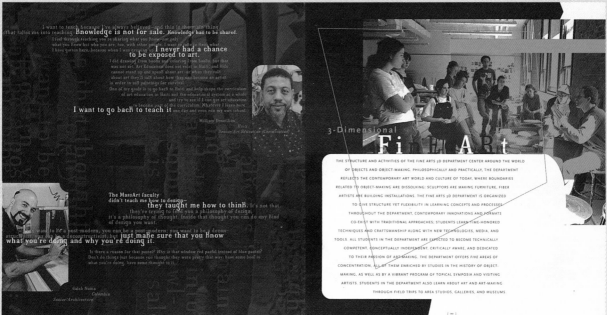

Acuity 1.0 presents a system for determining the distance at which letterforms and symbols can be seen in any color combination for standard vision. Signifying the process of seeing, the image of an imposing human eye provides a visual centerpiece for the CD cover. The background colors and the hues assigned to the typography are influenced by the colors composing the eye. Contrast is achieved by using highly saturated colors compared to the softer colors of the eye.

TIP: To improve the legibility of type and backgrounds consisting of pure analogous colors, try lightening the value of the backgrounds. The tradeoff will result in a loss of overall brightness and intensity but a gain in legibility. The amount, size, and style of text type and the specific colors in use will guide your decisions.

1

Printed in red, the title *Acuity* bisects the eye, stretching from the pupil to the edge of the cornea. The treatment of the title is in effect a demonstration of the principles of visual acuity. The chosen typeface, size, and color enable optimal readability of the word from a distance of 12 to 14 inches. Beyond this distance, the title is difficult to impossible to read. While the specific hue and intensity of the letters provide sufficient contrast for overall readability of the word, certain letters are more legible than others. The *A*, for example, is more legible than the *t*, for there exists more contrast between this letter and its surrounding background. In general, the use of red contributes to striking color schemes, and it is a hue that is rarely confused with other hues.

2

Icons used to drive the software are pictured on the CD cover. These chromatic images are designed to represent specific software tools and functions. Not only do these depictions provide a clue about what is found in the actual software, they add a visual richness to the cover. The icons represent the following software functions: motion, typeface, type size, lighting, eyesight, reflection, color, and calculation (left to right).

3

The contrast between the violet and orange parts of the background is heightened by a stairstep edge aligned to the row of icons at the top of the cover. The stairstep pattern not only focuses attention on the dissonance between the two colors, it references the "building block" process unique to the software tools.

4

Pure red and violet stand one color apart on the color wheel for an analogous relationship. Text type on the CD cover appears in red on violet, a combination that is very harmonious. Due to lack of value contrast, however, combinations such as these should be used only for small amounts of text type. Compare the difference in legibility as the violet background progressively lightens in value.

Designed by
John T. Drew,
Tom Henderson,
Sarah Meyer, and
Matthew Zito

1995. All rights reserved.
demark of ELEVEN 5, Inc.

red on violet

red on violet

red on violet

red on violet

red on violet

1
3
11

Typefaces: Gill Sans, New Baskerville Italic

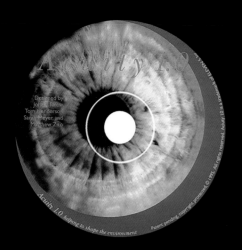

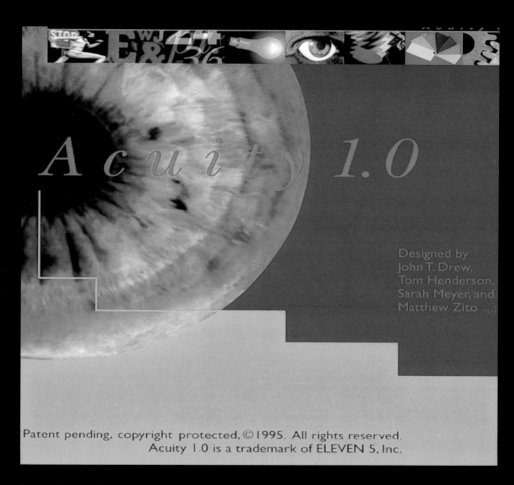

A saturated palette of the secondary hues of orange and violet contrasts with the muted tones of the eye image (bottom). The CD also incorporates the eye image as it corresponds to the overall design concept (top).

Design:
Mark Minelli
Pete Minelli
Lesley Kunikis
Brad Rhodes
Casey Reas
minelli design
CD Packaging Design:
Brad Rhodes

To achieve vibrant color and to multiply the actual number of colors available, try overprinting the transparent offset printing inks.

T I P :

An interactive CD package for the Art Institute of Boston is part of a greater identity system for the school. Bold typography, enhanced and articulated through a slightly offbeat color palette, characterizes each component of the system. A number of hybrid colors were created by overprinting red, green, and purple inks, a technique that also aided the designers in overcoming budget limitations. The approach to color and type suggests the creative and experimental nature of the art school without abandoning the clarity of factual information.

1
As shown in this example, two solid colors can be combined to generate a third hybrid hue that provides richness and depth.

2
The colors used for the CD packaging are the same ones used for the interactive "buttons" featured in the CD itself. These buttons are selected with the mouse to navigate information about the school. Enough contrast exists between the hues to easily distinguish one from another.

3
A sleeve within the cover holds the CD. On this panel, violet is used for highly legible type; yellow-green is used for the image.

5
A darker color is used for the CD itself. This somber hue relates to poetic images encountered while interacting with the program.

4
Color is distributed among the letterforms in a manner reminiscent of an abstract painting. Though only three colors are actually used in the printing, reversing some letters to appear as white and printing others over a color background achieves the appearance of several colors.

t30

t59

1

Typefaces: Bodoni, Rockwell

The CD cover shown front
and back reveals a
cacophonic mixture of
typographic forms and
emotive, passionate color.

Design:
Clifford Stoltze
Stoltze Design
Design Assistance:
Peter Farrell
Heather Kramer
Illustrators:
Various

CD packaging

TIP:

Remember that the color of the paper upon which you print adds to the total color palette. Also, since most printing inks are transparent, paper color always affects the color of the inks.

Anon, a limited-edition compilation of art and music, includes two music CDs and a collection of 30 full-color postcards that are packaged in a natural cardboard container. Themes for the CDs are solar and lunar, which are introduced on the cover in the form of a diagram of the solar system. The two main colors used for the packaging are yellow for solar, silver for lunar, and black for text. The yellow and silver appear soft and delicate on their earthy background, an effect accentuated by flourishes of gently curving calligraphy.

1

On the cover, type and images printed in yellow, silver, and black overlap to create a complex and delicate motif. *Anon* is printed in black to clearly identify the title. Despite the complexity of the layers, each is clearly distinguished from the next.

 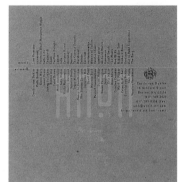

2

A red-orange band binding the package together repeats the title, introduces the contents of the package, and brings warmth to the entire presentation.

3

Enlarged portions of the solar system diagram found on the cover and the title *Anon* in calligraphic letters are reversed from white to reveal the inherent silver cast of the CD.

k10

k3

5

Typefaces: Calvino, Gangly

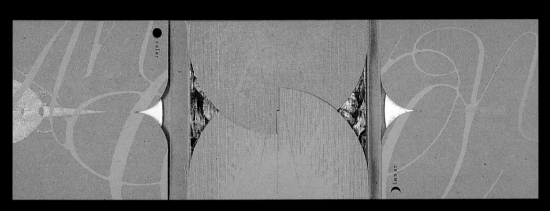

The packaging is a statement of contrasting forms, materials, and colors: the square shape of the container and the round diecut flaps representing the sun and moon; the raw neutrality of the packaging material and the elegance of the yellow and silver inks; and the title *Anon* presented in both curvilinear calligraphy and rectilinear type.

Design:
Jack Anderson
Lisa Cerveny
Jana Wilson
Suzanne Haddon
Hornall Anderson Design
Works, Inc.
Art Direction:
Jack Anderson
Copy Writer:
Karen Wilson

For GNA Power Annuities, bold colors are used to depict the concept of "power." In fact, the design staff refers to specialty color mixes as Power Red, Power Orange, Power Gold, etc. These colors are forceful because of their intensity and slightly dark value. Also contributing to their strength is the extent to which they are used. Large, overlapping letters and numerals appearing in the power colors dynamically engage large areas of space within printed materials.

1
The large letters and numerals overlap one another with precision, subdividing the space into elegant, abstract shapes. The overlapping letters appear transparent as color changes in value at points of intersection.

2
While the same colors are used throughout the program, they are applied differently to each piece of communication. This technique not only establishes variety within the system, it helps to distinguish the various materials as well.

POWER

3
On the inside of a brochure, letters alternate in color to emphasize the word *POWER*.

4
For optimum readability, black text always appears on lighter values of the colors.

k10
s28
t54
t20
s3
3

Typefaces: MS Gothic, Sabon

The cover of a folder containing information about the company typifies the use of the power colors and the monumental letters and numbers that expand beyond the borders. This palette consists of the tertiary hues red-orange, yellow-orange, and red-violet.

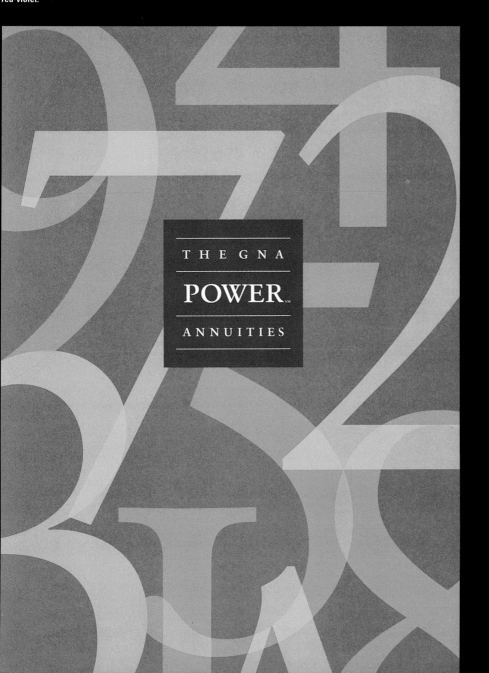

THE GNA

POWER SM

ANNUITIES

A photograph of sky and clouds serves as a poetic backdrop for this cover of *exp.* magazine. The sun establishes a dramatic focal point that draws attention to the magazine's vivid red title. The cottony appearance of the clouds provokes a strong contrast with rectilinear shapes that provide an organizational framework for the typography. The shapes appear as tinted glass panes with hues that intensify areas of the achromatic photograph. Juxtaposed with the sky, the color intensifies the illusion of three-dimensionality and creates a mood of contemplation and mystery.

TIP: Using transparent color provides an effective way of synthesizing type and photographs. However, be aware that an increase in transparency usually translates into a decrease in legibility. This technique works best for display rather than text type.

1
The computer enabled the designer to precisely adjust the color opacity in the rectangular shapes and letterforms. More opacity results in less transparency, while less opacity results in more transparency.

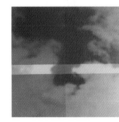

2
When reversing type from a background photograph, it is essential that the background is dark enough to ensure readability. This is a matter of contrast: if the background is too light, the type will appear too faint and therefore less readable.

3
Many different typographic manipulations can be used to separate and emphasize information, including the use of different typefaces and type weights. Assigning different colors to typographic parts is also an effective means to emphasize one element over another. Here, the word *Three* and the date *1996* achieve prominence through color.

Mental Hat Racks
Richard Saul Wurman

The Legacy of Gestalt Psychology
Max Wertheimer and Kurt Koffka

4
A spread from the magazine's feature story utilizes the sky photograph, linking the cover and magazine interior. An image of a woman with the word *psychology* overlapping her forehead illustrates the topic of Gestalt psychology. The use of transparent color keeps the look of the magazine consistent.

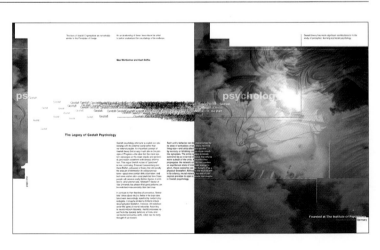

Typeface: Helvetica

3

Volume three
March/April 1996

exp.

exp.magazine
the design **experience**

Mental Hat Racks
Richard Saul Wurman

The Legacy of Gestalt Psychology
Max Wertheimer and Kurt Koffka

Dedicated to the study and discussion
of the graphic design experience. It is be-
lieved that we remember through experience and understand information in a
more concise manner through interaction.

In the case of graphic design, it must
not operate merely as a vehicle that sends
the message to the receiver, but stand
as a cultural artifact which allows one to
experience information in the fullest sense.

Design:
Jerry Hutchinson
Hutchinson Associates, Inc.

The primary purpose of this magazine advertisement is to demonstrate the high-quality printing capabilities of Dupli-Graphic. A closely cropped blue flower – exquisite, graceful, and subtly textured – serves as the ad's centerpiece. The ad is divided into halves; the top half contains the flower, and the bottom half displays a deep black field. The hardness of the black accentuates the flower's softness, and together the two parts form a rich and complementary whole. The flower and its blue hue suggest elegance, sophistication, and beauty.

TIP: You can use typographic color as achieved through type style and spacing to give your design variety and vigor and to establish an ordered hierarchy among parts.

1

Within the ad's black rectangle, two blocks of text type reversed to appear as white are different in tone and luminescence. Referred to as typographic "color" (see page 33), any number of tones can be created by controlling typeface, type weight, spacing, and type size. In this example, text units differ distinctly in brightness and tone.

color and type

color and type

color and type

c o l o r   a n d   t y p e

2

At first glance the advertisement is a statement of blue and black only, but closer observation reveals a subtle yellow-green hue emanating from the center of the flower and in the letters *Dupli*. Finding relationships between even subtle colors within a design can provide nuance and color harmony.

3

Blue is also represented in Dupli-Graphic's logotype. The color begins at the top of a circle, and gradually fades as it moves in a clockwise direction. Together with the color gradation, the symbol abstractly refers to the printing process.

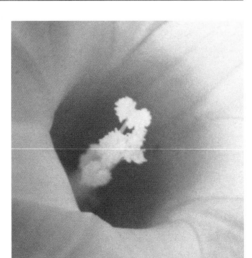

Dupli

w
s23
s43
k10

Typefaces: Akzidenz Grotesk, Akzidenz Grotesk Extended

Dupli-Graphic

Serving the design community since 1948

High end electronic pre-press services

Complete electronic and conventional image assembly

Color scanning

Sheetfed printing, one through five colors

Complete bindery service

Die cutting and embossing

Old world letterpress capabilities

48 years of dedication to fine quality sheetfed printing. Single through five color capabilities.

3628 North Lincoln Avenue
Chicago, Illinois 60613

t. 312 549 5285
f. 312 549 4222
e. print@dupli.com
w. www.dupli.com

Where the advertisement's upper and lower halves join at the center, an edge is formed that establishes the design's central axis. Small lines of black type running vertically from the axis state the capabilities of the printing firm, unify the halves, and soften the hard edge.

Design:
Clifford Stoltze
Brett Snyder
Heather Kramer
Peter Farrell
Rebecca Fagan
Stoltze Design

TIP: When appropriate, choose color for type that mirrors the implied emotional and symbolic content of a message.

Postcards designed by Stoltze Design express the meanings of significant words through the poetic use of color and type. Entitled *Presents of Mind,* the cards are sent to friends and clients. The series offers a marvelous collection of creative color and type effects generated on the computer.

Content used for the cards are dictionary definitions of the selected words. The three colors used for the postcards include a glowing, phosphorescent orange; a subtle, metallic bronze; and a deep, oceanic blue-green. These colors possess rare qualities and join with type in a lively, chromatic concert.

1

One sees a "spark" in overlapping letters and fragmented oblique shapes. The definition of spark as "something set off by a sudden force" is emphasized over other definitions by appearing in bright orange instead of blue-green.

2

The word *passion* looks passionate through an emphatic layering of two contrasting typefaces and colors. "Flames" of passion appearing in the hot color flicker through a rectangular text block in cool blue-green.

3

The concept of purity ("free from what vitiates, weakens, or pollutes") is established by extracting the word from its environment and placing it upon a different color within a new environment .

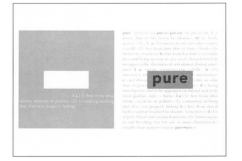

w

k2

s39

t10

Typefaces: various

overlapping elements demonstrates "harmony." Presenting the word in an elegant script and repeating it in a soft blend of mono-chromatic blue-greens reinforces the concept.

harmony

1 *archaic* : tuneful sound : MELODY 2 a : the combination of simultaneous musical notes in a chord b : the structure of music with respect to the composition and progression of chords c : the science and the structure, relation, and progression of chords

3 a : pleasing or congruent arrangement of parts <a painting exhibiting ~ of color and line> b : CORRESPONDENCE, ACCORD <lives in ~ with her neighbors> c : internal calm : TRANQUILLITY

4 a : an interweaving of different accounts into a single narrative b : a systematic arrangement of parallel literary passages (as of the Gospels) for the purpose of showing agreement or harmony

Postage stamp

Consider using warm colors when you wish to create impact. Most people respond emotionally to these hues of high intensity. There exists a fairly balanced distribution of warm and cool colors on the color wheel; however, people can physically see far more warm colors than cool ones.

T I P :

The *A* stamp is the official priority mail stamp of the Swiss Post Office. Typically, expensive priority stamps are given warm colors while less expensive stamps are assigned cooler colors. For this stamp, Jean-Benoît Lévy decided to primarily employ warm colors but also to introduce cool colors for contrast. The edges of three interlocking shapes suggest an uppercase *A*. Stripes placed at the edges of the planes clearly define the letterform. The trilogy of shapes forming the letter *A* represents the three co-dependent parts of the mailing process: message, sender, and receiver.

1

The pinwheel shapes of the stamp appear substantially warmer and luminescent as they hover over a complementary cool blue sky. Within two of the shapes, linear color blends of red and yellow provide a shimmering effect.

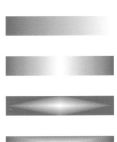

2

Color blends and fades are effectively used in the stamp design. Easily achieved with a computer, this device modulates the surface of a form, providing a sense of three-dimensionality. As shown here, blends and fades come in several varieties, including linear, mid-linear, diamond, and rectangular.

3

Printed on an envelope is a simplified variation of the *A* form. Here, the structure of the stamp is clearly revealed. Moving clockwise, the shapes appear in an analogous gradation of red, orange, and yellow. This logical gradation provides cohesiveness and unity among the colors. The three functions of the mailing process are presented in converging upper-case letters printed over the three rectilinear shapes. These terms, presented in three languages, appear as three different but closely related hues.

4

The vivid warm colors and crisp geometric design of the *A* stamp give it distinction among other stamps.

Typeface: Futura

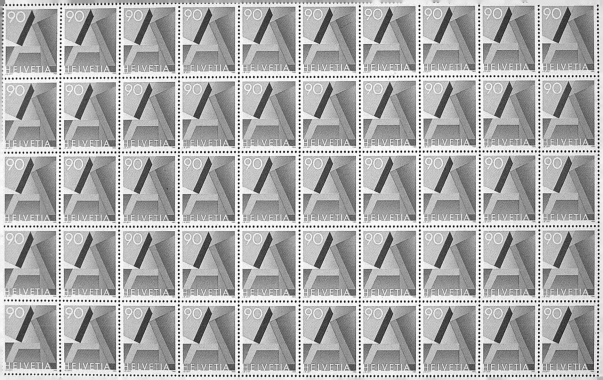

TIP: If you are limited to the use of black, white, and gray, remember that these neutral colors work best when type and background contrast significantly in value, and that type set as a darker value on a lighter value works better than the inverse.

An opera poster for *Ariadne auf Naxos* comes to life in a rhythmic orchestration of type and color. This poster demonstrates how color may serve both as a means to emphasize and de-emphasize parts of information and to symbolically portray content. The poster is divided into two zones: a top zone consisting of a warm gray rectangle and robust typography that introduces the event; and a bottom zone with additional information set in text type and a painting by Titian called *Bacchus and Ariadne*. The painting portrays the classical myth surrounding the content of the opera.

1

The name *Richard Strauss* and the title *Ariadne auf Naxos* appear together on the warm gray rectangle in approximately the same size. Making one of these elements white and the other black creates a subtle distinction in emphasis. As the black unit advances in space, the white unit recedes (top). When both elements are assigned the same color, they are nearly equal in emphasis (bottom).

Richard Strauss
Ariadne auf Naxos

Richard Strauss
Ariadne auf Naxos

2

This example demonstrates how as the background changes in value, the type elements change in emphasis.

Richard Strauss
Ariadne auf Naxos

Richard Strauss
Ariadne auf Naxos

Richard Strauss
Ariadne auf Naxos

3

Below the gray rectangle, a painting by Titian entitled *Bacchus and Ariadne* portrays the classical myth upon which the opera is based. The painting is split horizontally into halves with the top half printed in black and white, and the bottom half printed in full color. This device represents the two distinct acts of the opera – two related but separate parts. The first act is a discussion among the actors about writing and producing an opera; the second act is a performance by the actors of the opera discussed in the first act. The black and white division of the painting signifies the unrealized production; the full-color component suggests the operatic event in real time.

k3
k10
w

Typefaces: Garamond, Univers

Sinfonia
da Camera
Ian Hobson, music director

Ian Hobson, *conductor*
Nicholas DiVirgilio, *director*

Richard Strauss

Ariadne auf Naxos
A comic, chamber opera

Saturday March 30 1996 at 8:00pm
Foellinger Great Hall
Krannert Center for the Performing Arts
University of Illinois at Urbana-Champaign
Ticket information 217.333-6280

This performance is made possible through
the generosity of Richard and Rosann Noel.

Sinfonia da Camera appears under the auspices of the
University of Illinois at Urbana-Champaign in
association with the School of Music and the College
of Fine and Applied Arts.

The warmth of Titian's hues is reflected in the warm gray rectangle housing the title information. Using colors that possess similar properties helps to establish visual unity within a design.

The richness and brilliance of the four-color image is pronounced by the predominantly black, white, and gray surroundings. This vivid contrast not only brings visual impact to the poster, it also strengthens the underlying concept of the split image.

painting: Titian: *Bacchus and Ariadne*. 1520-23. National Gallery, London
design: David Colley
printing: Dupli-Graphix/Chicago

A poster for color studies in the Department of Design at Ohio State University demonstrates an interaction of two colors through color blends. The background progresses from red to blue, with the transition occurring at the center of the poster. A second, smaller field of color inverts the relationship, progressing from blue to red. The transition of this blend occurs also at the center. Through this color exercise, the essence of the poster's content is stated.

1

Because it is neutral, the white type on the background does not interfere with the rest of the color on the poster. Any other color would have changed the intended effect, which is to emphasize the red and blue blend. Compare the two examples shown here.

Notice how the addition of type in a third hue changes the effect and perception of the two background colors and therefore changes the entire color statement.

2

Perhaps the most intriguing aspect of the poster is the simultaneous interaction of the color blends and the new hue resulting from their mix. Aside from the pure delight of color blends, they can (given an appropriate context) signify change, transition, time, and movement. An array of blends are pictured here; study the hue resulting from the interaction of the first two hues.

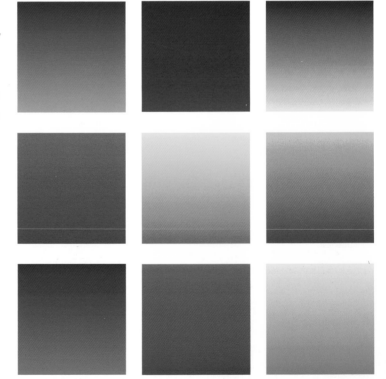

Typeface: Helvetica

Deeper Into Color

simultaneous contrast   vibration   transparency

programmed color   medial color

studies in complex color relationships in the Department of Design at the Ohio State University

For this poster announcing a summer program in architecture at Columbia University, designer Willi Kunz uses color to organize and structure the poster's space. Suggesting architectural spaces, yellow and black geometric forms asymmetrically frame the poster and house information related to the program. Resting above an image of New York City, a circular sphere suggesting the sun signifies the season in which the program is offered. The overall effect of the color is warm and optimistic.

TIP: If you are limited to the use of two colors, consider using a hue of darker value for type, and a hue of lighter value for background. This combination will optimize readability.

1

Although the black shape functions as a container for text type, it has a life and purpose of its own due to the strength of the black and the character of the shape. The boldness of the shape also calls attention to the information contained within it. Type can be placed into shapes of all kinds. Never, however, should the shapes distract from the message; they should in fact relate to it in some way. This shape refers to the architectural theme of the poster.

2

The juxtaposing arrangement of the black and yellow shapes (shown only as black shapes in the diagram) creates a third white shape. Together these interlocking forms establish the poster's organizational structure.

3

An effective transition from yellow to white is made in the poster by means of an intermediate series of yellow and white stripes. These alternating stripes read as a lighter yellow and soften the contrast between the yellow and white parts of the poster. Such transitions are often needed to bridge one color to another.

4

A light gray plane thrusting diagonally through the poster overlaps the sun motif and yellow shapes at the borders. This gives the plane a film-like, transparent quality.

York

w

k1

5

k10

Typeface: Univers

Introduction to Architecture

A Summer Studio in New York

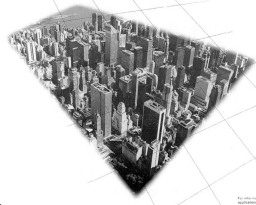

For information and applications write or call:

Office of Admissions – Introduction to Architecture Program
Columbia University
Graduate School
of Architecture, Planning, and Preservation
400 Avery Hall
New York, NY 10027
(212) 854-3414

A summer program giving university credit which introduces the student to aspects of the design, history, theory, and practice of architecture. The program is intended both for those without previous academic experience in design who are interested in architecture as a potential career, and for those with previous experience in architectural design who would like to develop additional studio design skills, perhaps in preparation for application to graduate school.

Courses are given in the studios of Avery Hall, home of Columbia University's world-renowned Graduate School of Architecture, Planning, and Preservation, on the Morningside Heights campus in New York City. Studios and seminar courses are taught by experienced architects and designers, coordinated and supervised by members of the faculty of the Graduate School. For those who may require it, housing is available on the University campus, with direct access to Avery Hall.

Students attend classes four days a week for five weeks, both morning and afternoon sessions. In the morning session, students are introduced to the fundamentals of architectural history and theory, structures, technology, and professional practice. Also, this course will introduce the student to the extraordinary city of New York, with its world famous collection of museums, cultural institutions, and architectural monuments. Lectures, seminar presentations, tours of architect's offices, and field trips to active building sites, museums, and famous works of architecture in New York City are led by the instructors.

In addition, students will attend a series of special lectures to be given by distinguished and renowned architects, including the following:

Kenneth Frampton
Architect; professor; author of "Modern Architecture, A Critical History"

Steven Holl
Architect; professor; winner of numerous Progressive Architecture Awards

James Stewart Polshek
Architect; professor; designer for the renovation of Carnegie Hall

Robert A. M. Stern
Architect; professor; author of "Pride of Place"

Bernard Tschumi
Architect; Dean, Columbia University; designer of the park "La Villette", Paris

In the afternoon, the students attend the design studio – an educational method unique to architecture – a place where students are given an intensive training in the skills and critical thinking involved in architectural design. Students, in small groups, work directly with studio instructors to develop their individual designs, which the students then present in periodic reviews or "juries", where they hear the comments and criticism of the invited architects and professors. The design projects given in studio are frequently situated in New York City, so that the student is able to apply the knowledge he or she has gained from the morning sessions. The development of supporting skills such as drawing and model-building is also included in the studio curriculum.

Together the studio and lectures present a comprehensive introduction to every aspect of architecture as it is practiced today. In addition, through the various field trips and tours, the student learns from the extraordinary examples of architectural and urban design in New York City, the world's preeminent center for architectural culture.

Program Director:
Thomas Hanrahan,
Architect, professor

Introduction to Architecture:
July 6 to August 6
Monday, Tuesday, Wednesday, Thursday
10:00am–5:00pm
3 credits, studio and seminar
Tuition for 1992: $1590
Housing on the Columbia University campus (if required): approximately 3000

Applications should include a transcript of the applicant's academic record, a resume summarizing education, employment, and other types of experience; and, where appropriate, examples of the applicant's design work. Also please include a $35 application fee (checks made out to: Columbia University).

Applications are due by June 30.

TIP:

When limited to the use of only two colors, select a pure hue and black. Most hues go well with black, and by screening and mixing the colors, a wide range of chromatic effects can be achieved.

A poster for the Master of Fine Arts program at Virginia Commonwealth University defies the limitations of using only two colors. The basic palette – yellow and black – represents the school's colors. This color combination is always very attractive, an attribute that is further enhanced through inventive spacing, screening, and layering of typographic elements. Indeed, this poster displays a wealth of two-color possibilities, and in doing so expresses the seriousness, involvement, and energy of the educational program.

1

While many typographic conventions are pushed aside for the sake of playful experimentation, critical information is set in black to preserve legibility.

2

In spite of the textured layering of type and color, black retains fidelity on the yellow-orange. Make note of how the heavier type appears black, and how the the lighter type appears gray.

3

A pattern of horizontal lines creates the effect of a lighter value of yellow-orange and draws attention to the adjacent photograph.

w

4

k10

Typeface: Univers

A large yellow dot provides a focal point for the poster. Lines of type radiate outward from the dot to encourage a search for information. While on the journey, color, type, and photographs give the reader a taste of the experiences offered by the program.

Design:
Nancy Skolos
Thomas Wedell
Skolos/Wedell
Photography:
Thomas Wedell

TIP: Black and red are always an excellent choice when limited to two colors. The stability of black and the energy of red offer a resonant contrast. From Renaissance books to modern advertising, this combination is ubiquitous and time tested.

This poster announces an exhibition that documents all 85 major shows of Marcel Duchamp's work. Because Duchamp was obsessed with the game of chess, this topic became the theme of the poster. Each of the show openings are set into blocks of type suggesting chess pieces and placed strategically around a metaphorical chess-board. The poster's typographic border is a repeated pattern of the word *DADA* used by Duchamp for a poster design for one of his shows in 1953.

1
The show listings, placed at various angles throughout the poster, appear in various combinations of red, black, and white. Unique use of color and type activates the space and supports the DADA theme of the poster. This detail reveals some of these combinations.

2
The border of the poster demonstrates a stimulating use of color and type. The letters *D* and *A* in the name *DUCHAMP* are slightly enlarged and assigned the color red. As the letters are repeated along the edges of the poster, the term *DADA,* the name of an art movement of the early 20th century, emerges.

3
Placed at identical angles, tucked behind forms within the underlying photograph, and presented in red, two large *M*s provide drama and focal points within the poster.

4
The large white letters in the name *Marcel* are carefully placed within the photo-graph to establish visual prominence. Placing the letters in a lighter section of the photograph would weaken them and render them less legible (see page 36).

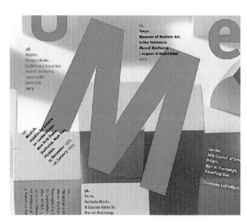

w

k10

2

Typefaces: Keedy Sans, Matrix, Meta

Design:
Nancy Skolos
Thomas Wedell
Skolos/Wedell
Photography:
Thomas Wedell

Poster

Use color for typographic support elements such as ruled lines, bars, leaders, bullets, and other dingbats (assorted symbols used with a type font) to effectively flag and emphasize important information.

TIP:

The annual Lyceum Fellowship Competition is a travelling fellowship for undergraduate students in architecture. The 1996 program focuses on the house as a design problem, challenging students to think about the need to design a home rather than working with a generic set of developer's plans. A piece of yellow tracing paper with a site plan peels away from the skeletal structure of a home to visually reflect the architect's role in the design process. Yellow elevates the temperature of the poster, providing a mood of comfort and warmth.

1

The Lyceum logotype is superimposed onto yellow tracing paper. The transparent layers of the logotype represent the stages of conceptualization. Typefaces used for the logotype are Serifa and Futura. Serifa is collegiate in appearance; Futura refers to modern architecture. Folds in the tracing paper generate different values of yellow and create a distinct three-dimensionality related to architecture. The alternating yellow shapes in this example suggest a similar dimensionality and the illusion of a strong light source.

2

The general distribution of colors divides the poster into two interlocking shapes and creates a structural framework for type and images. The spatial divisions are active yet proportionally pleasing.

3

Yellow bars help to articulate the architectural structure and serve also as flags that mark typographic elements.

4

Black type on a yellow background proves highly visible and readable, a color combination frequently used in highway signage. In fact, black type reads well on any of the lighter warm hues. Black on red does not provide optimum legibility because these two colors are too close in value.

w

k10

t18

Typefaces: Futura, Meta, Serifa

A Traveling Fellowship in Architecture

LYCEUM

Auburn University
The Boston Architectural Center
McGill University
Rhode Island School of Design
Rensselaer Polytechnic Institute
Southern California Institute of Architecture
University of Cincinnati

offered to
undergraduate
students
from
invited schools
who have
completed
five semesters
of study

COMPETITION

96

1996 Jury:

Jeremiah Eck, Chairperson
Architect
Boston, Massachusetts

Leslie Gill
Architect
New York, New York

Laura Hartman
Architect, Fernau & Hartman Architects
Berkeley, California

Mark Hutker
Architect
Martha's Vineyard, Massachusetts

Witold Rybczynski
Martin and Margie Meyerson
Professor of Urbanism
University of Pennsylvania

Prizes:

1st: $7,000
For Six Months
Travel Abroad

2nd $4,000
For Three Months
Travel Abroad

3rd: $1,000
Grant

Alternate:
Citation

House as Home/Profit or Place

The program identifies the student as a young, practicing Architect

relocated by a New England Developer looking for a new paradigm of the

American home to replace the ubiquitous center entrance "colonial"

The design proposal requires two house prototypes and a site plan

expressing a community of houses

Lyceum
Fellowship
Committee:

Jon Mckee
Chairman and Founder

Mark A. Hutker

Peter Vincent

Joseph Stinbowski

1000
Massachusetts
Avenue
Cambridge, MA
02138

House
as
Home

Design:
William Kochi
Kode Associates, Inc.
Photography:
William Kochi

TIP: When using color and type in publications, be consistent in the use of color for various typographic parts. For example, the small heads in this price guide are all presented in yellow.

This small price guide provides a helpful resource for LinoGraphics customers, and it demonstrates the company's many capabilities. Each page offers a visual surprise with romantic, muted travel photographs and type mingling in a layered and textured conversation. The concept of "official" is parodied throughout the book: the cover is printed in an "official" cool gray; an "official" safety pattern delicately marks the left edge of each spread; and the "official" corporate seal, emblazoned in vivid red on the opening spread, is combined as a ghosted image in each of the interior photographs.

1

A stunning attribute of the book is the textures achieved by layering the photographs and typographic elements. Sufficient hue and value contrast preserves the integrity of each element.

2

Color can be used to link information from one page to another. These two pages reveal how letters of the word *GUIDE* appear on two different pages. *GU* (on the first page) and *IDE* (on the second page) are printed in black, linking them together. *IDE* is also cleverly integrated into the word *IDENTITY* on the second page.

3

The book reveals tremendous variety in form and color. Each page or spread features something unique, such as the overlapping red, green, and blue letters *RGB* on the RGB Scans page.

4

Used in tandem, the red ruled lines and the black type contribute to highly readable charts despite all the effusive visual activity of the pages.

Typefaces: OCR-B, Rockwell, Styvesant

The cover, printed in cool gray and simple in design, sets the reader up for a major sensory surprise. Upon opening the book, the pages bloom with activity and color. Juxtaposing neutral colors with highly chromatic colors can – when proportioned carefully – dazzle and delight the eye. A red colon at the right edge of the cover contrasts with the gray, appearing most luminescent because of its neutral surroundings. Though the smallest element on the cover, it is the most prominent. The mark is located in the same position and color on each spread, inviting the reader to turn to the next page (right).

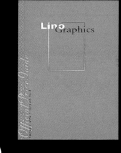

Lino Graphics

Kowloon, Hong Kong

Color Notes

rgb scans are closed-loop calibrated for output to fire 1000. all digital transparencies are imaged at res 50

Digital from postscript applications

		original	dupes
4"x5"		120	60
8"x10"		240	120

RGB

SCANS ⇒ FIRE 1000

DrumScans

	500 dpi	1000 dpi
4"x5"	75	125
8"x10"	125	175

Adobe PostScript

Rabat, Marocco

Production Note

image placements should include a laser proof noting size and positioning. complex silhouettes taking longer than 20 minutes are billed at $1.50 per minute.

Image Placement

	original
PER IMAGE	20

IMAGE PLACEMENT

SILHOU-ETTES

	original
PER IMAGE	30

On each spread the ghostlike remnants of the company's seal are reflected in computer-manipulated photographs (left).

Design:
David Collins
Judy Kirpich
Grafik Communications, Ltd.
Photography:
Pierre-Yves Goavec
Copy:
David Collins
Judy Kirpich

Promotional booklet

TIP:

As in this publication, use special color effects for type only when they contribute in some way to the design concept. If used for no apparent reason, special effects clutter and dilute a typographic message.

This promotional booklet showcases the photographic work of Pierre-Yves Goavec. Short phrases on the left-hand pages refer to the dynamic oppositional forces found in Goavec's work. These pages gleam with primary, secondary, and tertiary hues related to the photographs. They are intended to keep the book colorful but not at the expense of the photographs themselves. The type is computer manipulated to give the impression of projected light, a well-known trademark of Goavec.

1

To create an impression of projected light, type is blurred and shifted out of focus. The background color invades and softens the normally hard edges of the letters. In addition, the monochromatic type elements overlap as if projected in layers upon a surface.

3

To reference the process of projected light, the letter *G* (for Goavec) on the cover is revealed as a sequence of small diecut dots through which light could theoretically pass to form a pattern of shimmering color. Except for a yellow band running along the left edge, the cover is exclusively white – perhaps a statement of white light.

4

On the back cover, a logotype for Pierre-Yves Goavec consists of a vertical red capsule with white uppercase letters. Vertical slashes that divide lines of type at the top and the bottom of the cover mimic this element. Referred to as visual correspondence, this use of color establishes relationships among parts of the design.

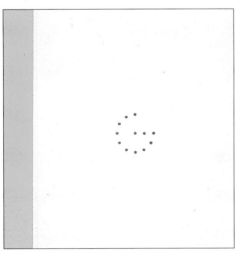

340 HARRIET STREET | SAN FRANCISCO, CA 94103

PIERRE-YVES GOAVEC

w

s42

s57

s2

10

s36

t20

2

The computer can generate blurred type, a special effect that is greatly influenced by the colors used, for tonal gradations occur within the letters.

Typefaces: Berkley, Myriad

Intensity
without
harshness

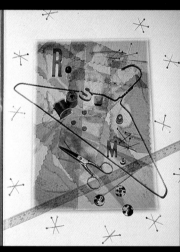

Randomness
without
chaos

Definition
without
edges

Three spreads from the booklet reveal the interrelatedness of the left- and right-hand pages. Colors for the left-hand pages are cued from the chromatic mix of colors in the adjacent photographs.

The design and color of this 45 RPM record album are sympathetic to the music of Minnow, the band featured on the album. Ambiguous and irregular shapes, an unusual typeface called Democratica, and a poetic organization of elements reflect the unique structure of Minnow's songs. Highly contrasting colors refer to the mood changes in the music. On the cover, small photos of numerals affixed to the band's instruments suggest a musical countdown (05, 04, 03, 02, 01) and contribute to the overall resonance of the design.

TIP:

Before selecting color, consider the moods and symbols it suggests. A few symbolic references are presented here:

Red: active, youthful, intense
Orange: exciting, spontaneous
Yellow: kinetic, upbeat
Green: fresh, healthy, hopeful
Blue: calm, trusting, strong
Violet: magical, imaginative

1

The emotion and mood of the band's music are established by the use of a split complementary color scheme. As described in chapter 2, this color scheme consists of a color and one or both of the colors on either side of its complement. Split complementary schemes are highly dynamic, as illustrated by the examples shown here. While only variations of the pure hues are shown, value adjustments in the colors would boost legibility when working with type.

2

Within the contrasting setting of split complementary colors, the use of very similar analogous hues such as orange, yellow, and yellow-green add a touch of subtlety and precision, another earmark of the band's music.

3

The two sides of the album cover are unified by reintroducing each of the split complementary colors as type. For example, the name *Minnow* appears on the yellow background in deep blue, while small text type appears in yellow on the blue. This weaving of color is illustrated in the diagram below.

4
5
s46

Typeface: Democratica

minnow

rod deems
nathan clague, vocals
patrick, bass
daniel guerre

01

recorded by ricky
tubb, deetunes-a-spa
cial thanks to patrick
kavanagh of hark for the
printing of this cover and to everyone who has
helped us in one way or anothers contact num
now at 13081 n franklin st. richmond va.
23220-(804)-353-7751

b
a
3.4 the mean, if ed s ply
the mean ted s ply

wings to fly

Design:
Jack Anderson
David Bates
Hornall Anderson Design
Works, Inc.
Art Direction:
Jack Anderson

Cf2GS is the acronym for the lengthy marketing communications firm's name Christiansen, Fritsch, Giersdorf, Grant, and Sperry, Inc. The creative use of the *2* for the two partners whose names begin with *G,* the innovative use of upper- and lower-case letters, and the incorporation of expressive color make this stationery system both unique and memorable. The elements of the logotype can appear in a serious and formal setting or in a more playful environment as purposes dictate.

TIP: If you wish to accentuate and preserve the purity of hues within a typographic design, this can be accomplished by placing them upon white, black, and neutral gray backgrounds.

1
The colors used for the letters of the logotype consist of warm gray, cool gray, and bright yellow. The yellow glows in the midst of the more neutral hues, acquiring a strong presence and providing the mark with distinction. Without the contrasting yellow hue, the color would be lackluster at best.

2
Contrasts of hue, value, and intensity infuse a design with visual vitality. Shown from left to right is a composition that progresses from monochromatic elements to the addition of tints and finally to the addition of different hues and values. In the last example, color harmony is achieved through the juxtaposition of the two warm elements and the two cool elements.

  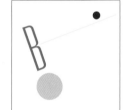

3
Typically, letterforms lie upon a stage of black, each acting out assigned roles (left). Sometimes, however, the letters behave playfully. Compare the front and back of the business card. To emphasize each partner equally, the largest letter of the last name is accentuated through size and position.

MARKETING
COMMUNICATIONS

c/2GS

DAVID GIERSDORF

1008
WESTERN AVE
SUITE 201
SEATTLE, WA
98104

206 223-6464
FAX 223-2765

4
For variety, background colors for stationery items alternate between the three established hues. For example, on the back of the letterhead, the background shifts from black to cool gray. The numeral *2,* which is normally presented in white, now appears in black.

W

t20

k1

k4

k10

Typefaces: Bodoni, Caslon, Futura, Copperplate

The season program for the Steppenwolf Theatre Company reverberates with startling color and typographic virtuosity. Contrasting combinations of tertiary colors appear in great variety throughout the program, echoing the drama and excitement of the theatre. Typographic treatments are painstakingly resolved, appearing as a cast of well-rehearsed and talented characters. The reader is held captive by the energy and wit of this publication.

TIP :

As illustrated in this program, energy, rhythm, and variety can be achieved within a publication if the specific concentration and allocation of color varies and shifts from page to page.

1

Selected spreads reveal the eloquent variety of the color and type.

2

The typographic configuration introducing the play *Everyman* demonstrates a crafted unification of type, image, and color. Divided into two colors – white and blue-violet – the title is both resonant and readable. Note also the precise alignments of the type and image.

3

A subscription form on the last page of the program uses color to organize information. Zoning type with color in this way makes the form easier to complete.

4

Plays presented within the program are identified by a system of vertical bands. The bands, split into two colors, contain the number and dates of each play.

w

t30

3

t53

k10

Typeface: Meta, Reactor

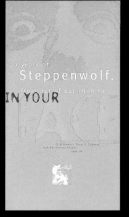

20 years of
Steppenwolf.
From out of our mind to

IN YOUR
FACE

(Steppenwolf Theatre Company
20th Anniversary Season
1995-96)

PLAY

3

FEBRUARY 14—MARCH 31, 1996

The Libertine

AMERICAN PREMIERE!

A PLAY BY STEPHEN JEFFREYS

Acclaimed Steppenwolf actor

John Malkovich

returns to the Chicago stage in this trenchant, witty portrait of the Earl of Rochester, the raconteur who inspired Etheridge's classic play "Man of Mode."

The Earl of Rochester delights in ravaging the noble fools of 1660's London with his rapier wit and merciless cynicism. His escapades with wine and women bring him celebrated notoriety, but he is not at all prepared to find truth and beauty in the world in the form of a young and talented actress—whose treachery may surpass even his own.

"I AM THE CYNIC OF OUR GOLDEN AGE. THIS BOUNTEOUS DISH WHICH OUR GREAT CHARLES AND OUR GREAT GOD HAVE PLACED BEFORE US SETS MY TEETH PERMANENTLY ON EDGE."

PHOTO: BRIGITTE LACOMBE

Yellow-green and blue-violet split an image of John Malkovich, intensifying the already provocative image. Typographic elements frame the eyes of the actor, calling attention to his piercing gaze.

Colorful wall graphics were designed to create public awareness of a historic site owned by The Council for America's First Freedom. This site will be the location of a reconstruction of Virginia's first capitol, a religious freedom study center, and a monument to religious freedom. At this location in 1786, Thomas Jefferson's Statute for Religious Freedom was approved by the Virginia General Assembly. This was the first time religious freedom was guaranteed to a people by law.

Wall graphics

TIP:

If you wish to give selected typographic elements precedence over other elements in an environment of pure hues and shades, try dressing them in white. This will thrust them towards the viewer and imbue them with commanding visual strength.

1

The rectilinear shapes of the walls provide a structural framework for the organization of the color and typography. On this wall the most vivid element is a vertical red bar enclosing Thomas Jefferson's name. The words of the statute, set in justified Helvetica type with generous leading, are white against a blue-green background. This luminous typography commands attention and worthily presents the message's content.

2

To avoid competition with the visual strength of the statute, the title typography is deliberately assigned less contrasting colors.

3

Commemorating the reconstruction of Virginia's first capitol at this site, a replica facade was built and placed upon a warehouse wall. An enormous initial capital *O*, set in yellow upon a deep blue-green background, rises like the sun to focus the reader's attention upon historic facts.

Typeface: Helvetica

Monumental typography set upon blazing walls separates historic site buildings from the surrounding city environ- ment. The pure hues of yellow, red, blue-green, and blue-violet provide startling contrast to the somber tones of the cityscape.

This CMYK color conversion chart provides the percentages of process colors used in examples throughout the book.

Column 1

	c	m	y	k
s5	100	100		80
s4	100	100		70
s3	100	100		50
s2	100	100		30
s1	100	100		10
1	100	100		
t5	90	80		
t4	70	65		
t3	55	50		
t2	30	30		
t1	20	15		
s10	80	100		80
s9	80	100		70
s8	80	100		50
s7	80	100		30
s6	80	100		10
2	80	100		
t10	65	80		
t9	50	65		
t8	40	50		
t7	30	35		
t6	20	20		
s15	60	100		80
s14	60	100		70
s13	60	100		50
s12	60	100		30
s11	60	100		10
3	60	100		
t15	50	80		
t14	40	65		
t13	30	50		
t12	20	35		
t11	15	20		

K table

	c	m	y	k
k10				100
k9				90
k8				80
k7				70
k6				60
k5				50
k4				40
k3				30
k2				20
k1				10
w				0

Column 2

	c	m	y	k
s20	40	100		80
s19	40	100		70
s18	40	100		50
s17	40	100		30
s16	40	100		10
4	40	100		
t20	30	80		
t19	25	65		
t18	20	50		
t17	10	35		
t16	5	25		
s25		100		80
s24		100		70
s23		100		50
s22		100		30
s21		100		10
5		100		
t25		80		
t24		65		
t23		50		
t22		35		
t21		25		
s30	55		100	80
s29	55		100	70
s28	55		100	50
s27	55		100	30
s26	55		100	10
6	55		100	
t30	40		80	
t29	30		65	
t28	20		50	
t27	15		35	
t26	10		20	

Column 3

	c	m	y	k
s35	85		85	80
s34	85		85	70
s33	85		85	50
s32	85		85	30
s31	85		85	10
7	85		85	
t35	75		70	
t34	65		55	
t33	55		45	
t32	35		35	
t31	25		20	
s40	100		40	80
s39	100		40	70
s38	100		40	50
s37	100		40	30
s36	100		40	10
8	100		40	
t40	90		35	
t39	70		30	
t38	55		25	
t37	40		20	
t36	25		10	
s45	100	55		80
s44	100	55		70
s43	100	55		50
s42	100	55		30
s41	100	55		10
9	100	50		
t45	85	45		
t44	65	40		
t43	50	35		
t42	40	25		
t41	25	10		

Column 4

	c	m	y	k
s50	100	85		80
s49	100	85		70
s48	100	85		50
s47	100	85		30
s46	100	85		10
10	100	85		
t50	90	75		
t49	70	65		
t48	55	50		
t47	40	35		
t46	25	25		
s55	75	100		80
s54	75	100		70
s53	75	100		50
s52	75	100		30
s51	75	100		10
11	75	100		
t55	60	85		
t54	45	70		
t53	35	55		
t52	25	40		
t51	15	30		
s60	40		100	80
s59	40		100	70
s58	40		100	50
s57	40		100	30
s56	40		100	10
12	40		100	
t60	35		80	
t59	30		65	
t58	25		50	
t57	15		35	
t56	5		20	

AND (Trafic Grafic)
Spalenvorstadt 11
4051 Basel
Switzerland

Cahan & Associates
818 Brannan Street, Suite 300
San Francisco, California 94103

David Colley
2820 East Grace Street
Richmond, Virginia 23223

Drenttel Doyle Partners
1123 Broadway
New York, New York 10010

Ernest Bernhardi
Communication Arts and Design
School of the Arts
Virginia Commonwealth
University
P.O. Box 842519
Richmond, Virginia 23284-2519

Grafik Communications, Ltd.
1199 N. Fairfax Street, Suite 700
Alexandria, Virginia 22314

**Hornall Anderson Design
Works, Inc.**
1008 Western, 6th Floor
Seattle, Washington 98104

Hutchinson Associates, Inc.
1147 West Ohio, Suite 305
Chicago, Illinois 60622

John T. Drew
University of Utah
Department of Art
AAC 161
Salt Lake City, Utah 84112

John Malinoski
815 Jessamine Street
Richmond, Virginia 23223

Kode Associates, Inc.
54 West 22 Street
New York, New York 10010-5811

Mark Oldach Design, Ltd.
3316 N. Lincoln Avenue
Chicago, Illinois 60657

Minelli Design
381 Congress Street, 5th Floor
Boston, Massachusetts 02210

Nathan Lambdin
Communication Arts and Design
School of the Arts
Virginia Commonwealth
University
P.O. Box 842519
Richmond, Virginia 23284-2519

Philip B. Meggs
10211 Windbluff Drive
Richmond, Virginia 23233

Planet Design Co.
605 Williamson Street
Madison, Wisconsin 53703

Rob Carter Design
2920 Glendower Circle
Midlothian, Virginia 23113

Sarah Meyer
University of Utah
Department of Art
AAC 161
Salt Lake City, Utah 84112

Scott Allison
Communication Arts and Design
School of the Arts
Virginia Commonwealth
University
P.O. Box 842519
Richmond, Virginia 23284-2519

Skolos/Wedell
529 Main Street
Charlestown, Massachusetts
02129

Stoltze Design
49 Melcher Street
Boston, Massachusetts 02210

Willi Kunz Associates, Inc.
2112 Broadway
New York, New York 10023

While writing and designing this book, several people offered generous assistance. I deeply appreciate the designers whose excellent work appears in Chapter 5. Despite the rigors of professional practice, they took time to provide materials, information, and permissions for reproduction. At Virginia Commonwealth University, John DeMao, Chairman of the Department of Communication Arts and Design, provided encouragement and support. At Rotovision SA, Brian Morris, Managing Director, and Angie Patchell, Senior Art Director, provided encouragement and guidance. Colleagues Philip Meggs and John Malinoski offered advice about content and design. With intelligence and sensitivity, Diana Lively read and copyedited the book. Molly Carter and Mindy Carter read the manuscript and made insightful suggestions. Mindy Carter also compiled the index. I greatly appreciate the commitment to quality and excellence of Alice Goh, Eileen Thong, and staff at Provision Ltd., Singapore. They make beautiful books. George Nan contributed impeccable photographic work. Jerry Bates and Joseph Dimiceli helped to solve technical problems as they arose. My wife, Sally Carter, offered endless encouraging words and made me laugh during difficult phases of the project.

Working with Computer Type 3 was typeset and designed on a Power Macintosh 7100/66. Software used includes QuarkXPress, FreeHand, Illustrator, and PhotoShop. Text throughout the book is set in the Univers family.

color

&type